QUILTING
through Life

Projects for the Mind, Body, and Soul

JULIA TETERS-ZEIGLER

Martingale®
& COMPANY

DEDICATION

> *"In quilting, as in life, the outcome of the whole rests in the value of each little piece."*
> —JO M. UHLMAN

I OWE A LIFETIME of gratitude to one of the most amazing women that I will probably ever meet! Margie Keck-Smith was truly a gift in my life when she became my speech therapist a few years ago. Not only did she believe in me, she pushed me to know that I could believe in myself. She gave me the tools to achieve, and it is an honor for me to dedicate this book to her.

That Patchwork Place® is an imprint of Martingale & Company®.

Quilting through Life: Projects for the Mind, Body, and Soul
© 2006 by Julia Teters-Zeigler

Martingale & Company
20205 144th Avenue NE
Woodinville, WA 98072-8478 USA
www.martingale-pub.com

Printed in China
11 10 09 08 07 06   8 7 6 5 4 3 2 1

MISSION STATEMENT

Dedicated to providing quality products and service to inspire creativity.

CREDITS

President · *Nancy J. Martin*
CEO · *Daniel J. Martin*
VP and General Manager · *Tom Wierzbicki*
Publisher · *Jane Hamada*
Editorial Director · *Mary V. Green*
Managing Editor · *Tina Cook*
Technical Editor · *Darra Williamson*
Copy Editor · *Durby Peterson*
Design Director · *Stan Green*
Illustrator · *Laurel Strand*
Cover Designer and Text Designer · *Trina Craig*
Photographer · *Brent Kane*

Library of Congress Cataloging-in-Publication Data
Teters-Zeigler, Julia.
    Quilting through life : projects for the mind, body, and soul / Julia Teters-Zeigler.
        p.   cm.
    ISBN 1-56477-640-9
    1. Patchwork—Patterns.   2. Quilting.   3. Patchwork quilts.
    4. Self-culture.   I. Title.
    TT835.T39 2006
    746.46'041—dc22
                                                    2005015997

CONTENTS

INTRODUCTION

WE ALL HAVE a tendency to take things for granted. We get so wrapped up in our jobs, errands that need to be done, and taxi service for our children that sometimes we lose sight of the core things that are important—I know I did! I believe that we all have so much to contribute from our own experiences; writing this book has been my outlet for "coming back" to quilting, for emerging into a new "normal" from the very active life I had prior to severe migraine-related health issues. There are people in our daily lives who are possibly hurting or perhaps need a boost, and I hope to give them the inspiration to live life to the fullest regardless of their situation!

> Life
> is raw material.
> We are artisans.
> We can sculpt our existence
> into something beautiful,
> or debase it into ugliness.
> It's in our hands.
> —CATHY BETTER

The insightful, yet gentle messages in this self-discovery quilting book can assist you in experiencing greater joy and fulfillment. Meander through the chapters, learning how to take better care of yourself, and thus giving yourself time to enjoy your passion: quilting!

I think we all let life in general lead us from day to day, so our days run into weeks, and weeks run into months, and we are left wishing we had more time. It has become a running joke among quilters that it will take a lifetime to create all the quilts we have in our heads or on our shelves waiting to be finished! To give you the time to quilt, as well as to inspire and challenge you to further your growth as a person and as a quiltmaker, I'd like to share with you some ideas for getting the most out of each day.

For a short time, let your mind, body, and soul travel with me on this journey. Along with quilts to make, each chapter is filled with ideas for identifying energy eliminators, home hassles, and daily destroyers, enabling you to set goals, put a plan in motion, and take action with confidence. This journey will apply to your personal self, your professional self, and—most importantly—your quilting self!

Express yourself, make memories, and—more than anything else—take time to enjoy what is important to you!

Life Is Not a Dress Rehearsal

EACH OF US is faced with the challenge of authoring our own lives. Start with the knowledge that you are precious. No success or failure can change that fact. How is your life going at this very moment? It may not be how you want it to be, but the good news is that as the author, you can write a new tomorrow!

There are limits to the time you have to live, but no limits on how you live your time. Every day you are free to choose between things that lift you up or things that drag you down.

Embrace experiences that can enrich your life. Absorb yourself in each opportunity. Find positives in every pursuit. Do it now, rather than waiting and wishing you had. Once your game is over and your life is nearing its end, it's too late. Now is the time to live each day. Now is the time to embrace your potential.

It's your life. If you don't manage your time, other people will manage it for you. For starters, pay close attention to the situations that cause you to lose energy or feel a knot in your stomach, or times when you simply need to sit down and have a good cry. Identify the people who drain your energy and the places where you need more space, more self-respect, or more personal power. Eliminate the things that drag you down. Embrace the things that lift you up!

Every night before I turn out the lights to sleep, I ask myself this question: Have I done everything that I can . . . . Have I done enough?
—LYNDON B. JOHNSON

Through Darkness Comes Light

The striking contrast between light and dark, coupled with the ever-popular color fuchsia, really causes the stars to "pop" in this bright, cheerful quilt.

Materials

Yardage is based on fabric that measures 40" wide after you have prewashed it and trimmed the selvages.

- 1⅞ yards *total* of assorted fuchsia fabrics for blocks and straight-grain binding
- 1⅛ yards of black solid for border
- 1⅛ yards *total* of assorted black-on-white prints for blocks
- 1⅛ yards of white striped fabric for pieced sashing
- 1 yard of black print for blocks and pieced sashing
- 3⅛ yards of fabric for backing
- 55" x 75" piece of batting

CUTTING

Cut all strips on the crosswise grain (from selvage to selvage).

From the assorted fuchsia fabrics, cut a *total* of:
- 192 squares, 2½" x 2½", in matching sets of 8
- 24 squares, 4½" x 4½"
- 2½"-wide strips to equal 256" for straight-grain binding

From the black print, cut:
- 10 strips, 2½" x 40"; subcut into:
    48 squares, 2½" x 2½"
    48 rectangles, 2½" x 4½"
- 3 strips, 1⅞" x 40"

From the assorted black-on-white prints, cut a *total* of:
- 48 rectangles, 2½" x 4½", in 24 matching sets of 2*
- 96 squares, 2½" x 2½", in 24 matching sets of 4*

*Cut these in 24 matching sets of 2 rectangles and 4 squares from the same fabric.

From the white striped fabric, cut:
- 3 strips, 1⅞" x 40"
- 3 strips, 2½" x 40"; subcut into 24 rectangles, 2½" x 4½"
- 4 strips, 4½" x 40"; subcut into 24 rectangles, 4½" x 6½"

From the black solid, cut:
- 6 strips, 6" x 40"

MAKING THE QUILT

Refer to "Quilting Basics" on page 72 for guidance as needed. Press seams in the direction indicated by the arrows.

MAKING THE STAR BLOCKS

1. Mark a diagonal line on the wrong side of each 2½" fuchsia square. Align a marked square right sides together with the left edge of each 2½" x 4½" black print rectangle and stitch directly on the marked line. Trim ¼" from the stitched line as shown; press. Make 48.

Make 48.

2. Repeat to stitch a matching 2½" fuchsia square to the right edge of each unit from step 1. Trim and press. Make 48.

Make 48.

3. Repeat steps 1 and 2 using the remaining 2½" fuchsia squares and the 2½" x 4½" black-on-white rectangles. Make 48.

Make 48.

Through Darkness Comes Light

Pieced by Julia Teters-Zeigler. Quilted by Sharon Welsh.

Finished quilt: 51½" x 71½" • Finished block: 8" x 8" • Skill level: intermediate

4. Arrange two matching units from step 2, two matching units from step 3, a 4½" fuchsia square, and four matching 2½" black-on-white squares in three rows as shown. Sew the units and squares into rows; press. Sew the rows together; press. Make 24.

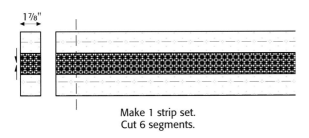

Make 24.

MAKING THE PIECED SASHING

1. Sew one 1⅞"-wide black print strip between two 1⅞"-wide white striped strips to make a strip set as shown; press. Cut six segments, 1⅞" wide.

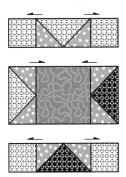

Make 1 strip set.
Cut 6 segments.

2. Sew one 1⅞"-wide white striped strip between two 1⅞"-wide black print strips to make a strip set as shown; press. Cut 12 segments, 1⅞" wide.

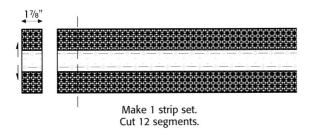

Make 1 strip set.
Cut 12 segments.

3. Sew one segment from step 1 between two segments from step 2 to make a nine-patch unit as shown; press. Make six. Refer to "Squaring Up Blocks" on page 76 and trim the units to 4½" x 4½".

Make 6.

4. Refer to steps 1 and 2 of "Making the Star Blocks" on page 7 and use the 2½" black print squares and the 2½" x 4½" white striped rectangles to make 24 units as shown.

Make 24.

5. Stitch a unit from step 4 to each 4½" x 6½" white striped rectangle as shown; press. Make 24.

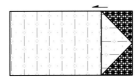

Make 24.

6. Stitch a nine-patch unit from step 3 between two units from step 5 as shown; press. Make six and label these sashing unit A. Label the remaining units from step 5 sashing unit B.

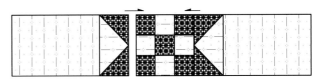

Sashing unit A.
Make 6.

ASSEMBLING THE QUILT

Following the assembly diagram below, arrange the blocks and pieced sashing units A and B as shown. Sew the blocks and units into rows; press. Sew the rows together. Press the seams open.

Assembly diagram

ADDING THE BORDER

Refer to the photo on page 8 as needed.

1. Sew the 6" x 40" black solid border strips together end to end to make a continuous 6"-wide strip; press the seams to one side. Cut two strips, 6" x 60½", and two strips, 6" x 51½".

2. Sew the 6" x 60½" border strips to the sides of the quilt. Press the seams toward the border. Sew the 6" x 51½" border strips to the top and bottom; press.

FINISHING THE QUILT

For detailed instructions on finishing techniques, refer to "Quilting Basics" on page 72.

1. Cut and piece the backing so it is 4" larger than the quilt. Layer the backing (with the seam running horizontally), batting, and quilt top. Baste the quilt in preparation for quilting.

2. Hand or machine quilt as desired. The quilt shown is quilted with a simple swirl pattern in each fuchsia star and stippling in the white areas. The border is stitched in a heavy swirl pattern with an exquisite fuchsia variegated thread.

3. Square up the quilt sandwich to prepare for binding. Sew the 2½"-wide fuchsia strips together end to end. Press the seams to one side. Refer to steps 4–8 of "Making and Adding Binding" on page 77 and use the fuchsia strip to bind the quilt.

4. Don't forget to make a label! Sometimes I like to use leftover fabrics to make another block for the label.

Quilt plan

Create a quiet space—time to think and take the small steps toward your goal. It may be sitting at your sewing machine. (That is where I spend a lot of my time thinking.) It may be soaking in a hot bath or working out the kinks with meditation, but set aside time for you! Even if it's only 15 minutes a day, have some quality time just for you.

Relaxing Chamomile Milk Bath

4 cups powdered milk
½ cup dried chamomile or
5 bags chamomile tea

Mix the 2 ingredients and place in a pretty glass jar. When you are ready to use it, pour 1 cup of milk-bath powder into 1 cup of boiling water. Let it steep for 20 minutes, and then strain and pour it into your bath. Relax!

Chamomile promotes general relaxation, and what a luxurious way to relax—
a nice hot chamomile milk bath. This recipe is so very simple, and the end result
is tranquil and soothing.

Getting
an idea should be
like sitting down on
a pin; it should make
you jump up and
do something.
—E. L. SIMPSON

Awakening the Soul

The commanding colors in this quilt, along with the striking design, will awaken your soul. The straightforward components of flying geese and strip sets make this an eye-catching project.

Materials

Yardage is based on fabric that measures 40" wide after you have prewashed it and trimmed the selvages.

- 4¾ yards of gold medium-scale floral for blocks, setting square, setting triangles, and outer border
- 3 yards of black small-scale print for blocks, flat piping, inner border, and binding
- 2⅜ yards of gold hand-dyed fabric for blocks
- 1⅝ yards of burgundy print for blocks and border corner squares
- 8 yards of fabric for backing
- 96" x 96" piece of batting

CUTTING

Cut all strips on the crosswise grain (from selvage to selvage).

From the burgundy print, cut:

- 17 strips, 2½" x 40"
- 1 strip, 7½" x 40"; subcut into 4 squares, 7½" x 7½"

From the gold hand-dyed fabric, cut:

- 30 strips, 2½" x 40"

From the black small-scale print, cut:

- 12 strips, 2½" x 40"; subcut into:
    128 squares, 2½" x 2½"
    32 rectangles, 2½" x 4½"
- 8 strips, 1" x 6½"
- 8 strips, 1" x 10½"
- 8 strips, 2⅜" x 40"
- 8 strips, 1½" x 40"

From the gold medium-scale floral, cut:

- 12 strips, 2½" x 40"; subcut into:
    64 rectangles, 2½" x 4½"
    64 squares, 2½" x 2½"
- 1 strip, 6½" x 40"; subcut into 4 squares, 6½" x 6½"
- 1 square, 22½" x 22½"
- 1 square, 32⅜" x 32⅜"; cut twice diagonally to yield 4 side setting triangles
- 2 squares, 16½" x 16½"; cut once diagonally to yield 2 corner setting triangles (4 total)
- 8 strips, 7½" x 40"

MAKING THE QUILT

Refer to "Quilting Basics" on page 72 for guidance as needed. Press seams in the direction indicated by the arrows.

MAKING THE BLOCKS

1. Sew one 2½" x 40" burgundy strip between two 2½" x 40" gold hand-dyed strips to make a strip set as shown; press. Make six strip sets and cut them into 88 segments, 2½" wide.

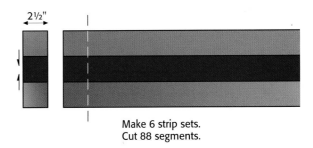

2½"

Make 6 strip sets.
Cut 88 segments.

2. Sew one 2½" x 40" burgundy strip and two 2½" x 40" gold hand-dyed strips to make a strip set as shown; press. Make eight strip sets and cut them into 128 segments, 2½" wide.

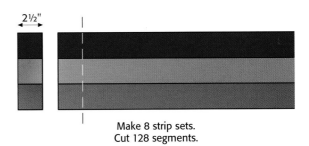

2½"

Make 8 strip sets.
Cut 128 segments.

AWAKENING THE SOUL
Pieced by Julia Teters-Zeigler. Quilted by Rose Flannigan.
FINISHED QUILT: 92½" x 92½" • FINISHED BLOCK: 22" x 22" • SKILL LEVEL: advanced

3. Sew one segment from step 1 between two segments from step 2, carefully arranging the segments to make a nine-patch unit as shown. Make 64. Set the leftover segments aside.

Make 64.

4. Sew the three remaining 2½" x 40" burgundy strips and the two remaining 2½" x 40" gold hand-dyed strips together, alternating them as shown to make a strip set. Cut eight segments, 2½" wide.

2½"

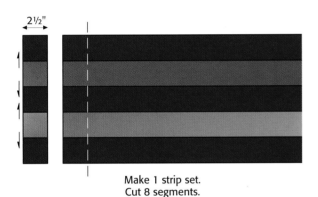

Make 1 strip set.
Cut 8 segments.

5. Mark a diagonal line on the wrong side of each 2½" black square. Align a marked square right sides together with the left edge of each 2½" x 4½" gold floral rectangle and stitch directly on the marked line. Trim ¼" from the stitched line as shown; press. Make 64.

Make 64.

6. Repeat to stitch a marked 2½" black square to the right edge of each unit from step 5. Trim and press. Make 64.

Make 64.

7. Repeat steps 5 and 6, using the 2½" gold floral squares and the 2½" x 4½" black rectangles. Make 32.

Make 32.

8. Arrange two units from step 6 and one unit from step 7 in a vertical row as shown. Stitch the units together; press. Make 32.

Make 32.

9. Stitch a remaining segment from step 3 between two units from step 8 as shown; press. Make 16.

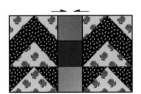

Make 16.

10. Press each 1" x 6½" black strip in half lengthwise with wrong sides together to create a flat-piping strip. Repeat with each 1" x 10½" black strip. Make eight of each.

11. With raw edges aligned and right sides together, sandwich a 1" x 6½" flat-piping strip between a 6½" gold floral square and a leftover segment from step 3. Pin, stitch, and press. Repeat to sew a 1" x 6½" flat-piping strip and a leftover segment from step 3 to the opposite side of the square; press. Make four.

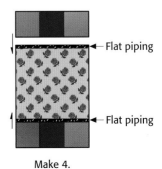

← Flat piping

← Flat piping

Make 4.

12. Repeat to sew a 1" x 10½" flat-piping strip and a segment from step 4 to the remaining sides of each unit from step 11 as shown; press. Make four.

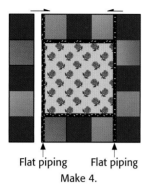

Flat piping   Flat piping
Make 4.

13. Stitch units from step 9 to opposite sides of each unit from step 12 as shown; press. Make four.

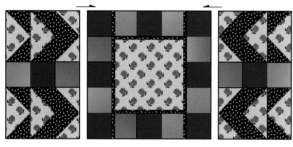

Make 4.

14. Arrange two units from step 3 and a remaining unit from step 9, taking care to orient the units as shown. Stitch the units together; press. Make eight.

Make 8.

15. Stitch a unit from step 14 to the remaining sides of the unit from step 13; press as shown above right. Make four. Refer to "Squaring Up Blocks" on page 76 and carefully square up each unit to 22½" x 22½".

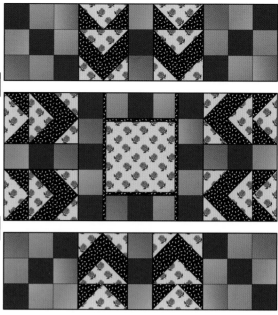

Make 4.

ASSEMBLING THE QUILT

1. Following the assembly diagram below, arrange the blocks, the 22½" gold floral square, and the gold floral side and corner setting triangles in diagonal rows as shown. Sew the blocks and side setting triangles into diagonal rows. Press the seams away from the pieced blocks. Add the corner setting triangles; press.

Assembly diagram

2. Sew the rows together and press the seams open. Square up the quilt top to measure 62¾" x 62¾".

BODY

Find time somewhere in your day for physical activity. Making this time will improve your heart and respiratory fitness, your mood, and your blood pressure—and it will reduce body fat! There are many ways that you can work physical activity into your day without taking precious extra time.

- Park your car at the end of the parking lot and walk to your destination.
- Take the stairs instead of the elevator.
- Rake leaves on a sunny day instead of using the leaf blower.
- Mow the lawn—it's a great calorie burner!
- Take the dog for a long walk when you get home from work.

I try to walk daily. Generally, I walk with some girls in the neighborhood who have welcomed me with open hearts to share laughter, stories, experiences, and sometimes sadness. They call themselves the Glenmore Girls. On the days that I walk with them, I feel inspired and lighthearted.

SOUL

Make an appointment with yourself. Mark it on your calendar—a retreat day for you to quilt. Invite a friend over to enjoy the day with you. If you take time for yourself, your soul will be filled and you will be able to accomplish more!

Adding the Borders

Refer to the photo on page 14 as needed.

1. Sew two 2⅜" x 40" black strips together end to end and trim to measure 2⅜" x 62¾". Make two and sew to the top and bottom of the quilt. Press the seams toward the border.

2. Sew two 2⅜" x 40" black strips together end to end and trim to measure 2⅜" x 66½". Make two and sew to the sides of the quilt; press.

3. Sew 11 nine-patch units to make a border unit, taking care to orient the nine-patch units as shown. Press the seams to one side. Make two and sew to the top and bottom of the quilt. Press the seams toward the black inner border.

Make 2.

4. Sew 13 nine-patch units to make a border unit, taking care to orient the nine-patch units as shown; press. Make two and sew to the sides of the quilt; press.

Make 2.

5. Sew two 1½" x 40" black strips together end to end and trim to measure 1½" x 78½". Fold in half lengthwise with wrong sides together and press to make a flat-piping strip. Make four.

6. Sew two 7½" x 40" gold floral strips together end to end and trim to measure 1½" x 78½". Make four.

7. With raw edges aligned and right sides together, sandwich a pressed flat-piping strip between the top edge of the quilt and one trimmed border strip. Pin and stitch. Press the seams toward the new border. Repeat to sew a flat-piping strip and trimmed border strip to the bottom edge of the quilt.

8. With raw edges aligned, use a ⅛"-wide seam to baste a remaining flat-piping strip right sides together with a remaining border strip. Sew a 7½" burgundy square to each end of the basted strip as shown; press. Make two. Sew a border strip to the sides of the quilt; press.

Make 2.

Quilt plan

Finishing the Quilt

For detailed instructions on finishing techniques, refer to "Quilting Basics" on page 72.

1. Cut and piece the backing so it is 4" larger than the quilt top. Layer the backing, batting, and quilt top. Baste the quilt in preparation for quilting.

2. Hand or machine quilt as desired. The quilt shown is quilted primarily with straight lines so the eye is not distracted from the intricate blocks. Sometimes simplicity in the quilting makes the quilt more appealing!

3. Square up the quilt sandwich to prepare for binding. Refer to "Making and Adding Binding" on page 77 and use the remaining black fabric to make 380" of bias binding. Use the binding to finish the edges of the quilt.

4. Don't forget to make a label! Sometimes I like to use leftover fabrics to make another block for the label.

Courage to Change

PERSONAL CHANGE HAPPENS through a journey of discovery. Discovery is learning, and the only prerequisite to learning is willingness!

The only constant is change—you can count on that. We live in an ever-changing universe: the cells in our bodies are replaced every seven years, and the seasons change as do governments, businesses, cultures, jobs, friends, and relationships.

Unfortunately, it is our nature to resist change of any kind. The fear of change and the fear of the unknown are so strong in some people that they remain in unfulfilling relationships, unhealthy environments, dead-end jobs, and many other self-destructive situations rather than facing the unknown. If you want a successful, happy, and productive life, you must learn to accept—even embrace—change!

You may be affected by outside forces, but even so, it's you who will decide how to turn things around. It can be difficult! We are comfortable with the status quo, going along our path, feeling fine, and then all of a sudden—*blast*—something happens to turn things upside down. The catalyst can be as minor as rain on your vacation or sewing for an hour only to realize your seam ripper is the only thing that will fix the mistakes you've made. It can be something as serious as a change in your health, your job, your home—or the loss of a loved one. Whatever the situation or circumstance, we must learn to handle change or it may immobilize us.

When one door of happiness closes, another opens; but often we look so long at the closed
door that we do not see the one which has been opened for us.
—HELEN KELLER

Courage
is the price that
life exacts for
granting peace.
—AMELIA EARHART

Wheels in Motion

The energetic movement of this stunning batik quilt takes your eye from the star that you sew to the stars that are created as the blocks are joined. Be courageous and challenge yourself. Get your wheels in motion!

Materials

Yardage is based on fabric that measures 40" wide after you have prewashed it and trimmed the selvages.

- 2⅞ yards of purple-and-orange bamboo batik for outer border and outer-border corner squares
- 2⅛ yards of cream batik for blocks
- 1⅝ yards of deep purple batik for blocks, flat piping, inner-border corner squares, and binding
- 1 yard of orange batik for blocks and inner border
- ⅞ yard of purple small-scale batik for blocks
- ¼ yard of cocoa multicolored batik for blocks
- 4½ yards of fabric for backing
- 80" x 80" piece of batting

CUTTING

Cut all strips on the crosswise grain (from selvage to selvage).

From the cream batik, cut:
- 3 strips, 1½" x 40"
- 2 strips, 3⅞" x 40"; subcut into 18 squares, 3⅞" x 3⅞". Cut each square once diagonally to yield 2 half-square triangles (36 total).
- 9 strips, 3" x 40"; subcut into 108 squares, 3" x 3"
- 5 strips, 2⅝" x 40"; subcut into 36 rectangles, 2⅝" x 4¾"
- 5 strips, 4¾" x 40"; subcut into 36 squares, 4¾" x 4¾"

From the deep purple batik, cut:
- 9 strips, 1½" x 40"
- 4 squares, 2½" x 2½"

From the cocoa multicolored batik, cut:
- 2 strips, 3" x 40"; subcut into 18 squares, 3" x 3". Cut each square once diagonally to yield 2 half-square triangles (36 total).

From the orange batik, cut:
- 2 strips, 5⅛" x 40"; subcut into 18 squares, 5⅛" x 5⅛". Cut each square once diagonally to yield 2 half-square triangles (36 total).
- 8 strips, 2½" x 40"; subcut 2 of the strips into 8 strips, 2½" x 7"

From the purple small-scale batik, cut:
- 9 strips, 3" x 40"; subcut into 108 squares, 3" x 3"

From the purple-and-orange bamboo batik, cut:
- 6 strips, 10½" x 40"
- 2 strips, 2½" x 40"; subcut into 8 strips, 2½" x 6"
- 4 squares, 10½" x 10½"

MAKING THE QUILT

Refer to "Quilting Basics" on page 72 for guidance as needed. Press seams in the direction indicated by the arrows.

MAKING THE BLOCKS

1. Sew one 1½" x 40" cream strip between two 1½" x 40" deep purple strips to make a strip set as shown; press. Cut 18 segments, 1½" wide.

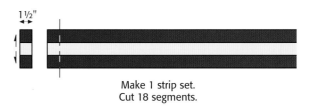

1½"

Make 1 strip set.
Cut 18 segments.

2. Sew one 1½" x 40" deep purple strip between two 1½" x 40" cream strips to make a strip set as shown; press. Cut nine segments, 1½" wide.

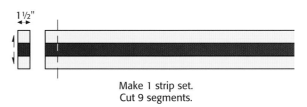

1½"

Make 1 strip set.
Cut 9 segments.

WHEELS IN MOTION

Pieced by Julia Teters-Zeigler. Machine quilted by Penny Virag.

FINISHED QUILT: 75½" x 75 ½" • FINISHED BLOCK: 17" x 17" • SKILL LEVEL: intermediate

3. Sew one segment from step 2 between two segments from step 1 to make a nine-patch unit as shown; press. Make nine.

Make 9.

4. Stitch cocoa multicolored half-square triangles to opposite sides of each nine-patch unit from step 3 as shown; press. Repeat to sew triangles to the remaining sides of the unit; press. Make nine. Refer to "Squaring Up Blocks" on page 76 and trim the units to 4¾" x 4¾".

Make 9.

5. Repeat step 4 to stitch cream half-square triangles to all four sides of each unit from step 4 as shown; press. Make nine. Refer to "Squaring Up Blocks" on page 76 and trim the units to 6½" x 6½".

Make 9.

6. Repeat step 4 to stitch orange half-square triangles to all four sides of each unit from step 5 as shown; press. Make nine. Refer to "Squaring Up Blocks" on page 76 and trim the units to 9" x 9".

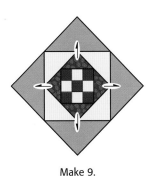

Make 9.

7. Mark a diagonal line on the wrong side of each 3" cream square. Place each marked square right sides together with a 3" purple small-scale batik square. Stitch ¼" from the marked line on both sides as shown. Cut on the marked line to make two half-square-triangle units; press. Make 216. Square up each unit to 2⅝" x 2⅝".

Make 216.

8. Arrange and stitch four half-square-triangle units from step 7 to make a horizontal row as shown. Press the seams open to eliminate bulk. Make 36.

Make 36.

9. Stitch a 2⅝" x 4¾" cream rectangle between two half-square-triangle units from step 7 as shown; press. Make 36.

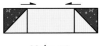

Make 36.

10. Stitch a unit from step 8 to a unit from step 9 as shown, matching the seams. Press the seams open. Make 36.

Make 36.

11. Stitch a unit from step 6 between two units from step 10 as shown. Press the seams open. Make nine.

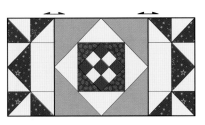

Make 9.

12.   Stitch a unit from step 10 between two 4¾" cream squares as shown; press. Make 18.

Make 18.

13.   Stitch each unit from step 11 between two units from step 12 as shown; press. Make nine.

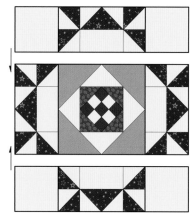

Make 9.

ASSEMBLING THE QUILT

Following the assembly diagram below, arrange the blocks in three horizontal rows of three blocks each. Sew the blocks into rows. Press the seams in opposite directions from row to row. Sew the rows together; press. Square up the quilt top to measure 51½" x 51½".

Assembly diagram

ADDING THE BORDERS

Refer to the photo on page 22 as needed.

1.   Sew the remaining 1½" x 40" deep purple strips together end to end to make one continuous strip. Cut four strips, 1½" x 51½". Fold each strip in half lengthwise with wrong sides together and press to make a flat-piping strip.

2.   Sew the 2½" x 40" orange strips together end to end. Cut four 2½" x 51½" inner-border strips.

3.   With raw edges aligned and right sides together, sandwich a pressed flat-piping strip between the top edge of the quilt and one inner-border strip. Pin and stitch. Press the seams toward the border. Repeat to sew a flat-piping strip and a border strip to the bottom edge of the quilt.

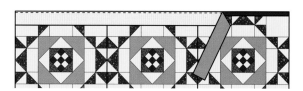

4.   With raw edges aligned, use a ⅛"-wide seam to baste a remaining flat-piping strip strip right sides together with a remaining inner-border strip. Stitch 2½" deep purple squares to opposite ends of the basted strip as shown; press. Make two. Sew to the sides of the quilt; press.

Make 2.

5.   Sew the 10½" x 40" purple-and-orange border strips together end to end to make one continuous strip. Cut four 10½" x 51½" outer-border strips.

6. With right sides together and the ends of the strips perpendicular to each other, stitch one 2½" x 6" purple-and-orange strip to one 2½" x 7" orange strip on the diagonal as shown. Trim ¼" from the stitched line and press. If necessary, trim from the purple-and-orange end so the piece measures 10½". Make four and four reversed as shown.

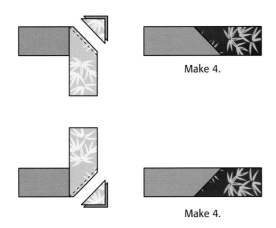

Make 4.

Make 4.

7. Stitch one of each unit from step 6 to opposite ends of a 10½" x 51½" outer-border strip; press. Make four. Sew one outer border to the top and bottom of the quilt.

8. Stitch 10½" purple-and-orange squares to opposite ends of the two remaining outer-border strips; press. Sew to the sides of the quilt; press.

Make 2.

FINISHING THE QUILT

For detailed instructions on finishing techniques, refer to "Quilting Basics" on page 72.

1. Cut and piece the backing so it is 4" larger than the quilt top. Layer the backing, batting, and quilt top. Baste in preparation for quilting.

2. Hand or machine quilt as desired. When selecting a quilting pattern, I like to use something subtle that highlights the fabrics in the quilt. The quilt shown is quilted with a variegated purple thread in a bamboo branch-and-leaf pattern both in the blocks and in the borders.

3. Square up the quilt sandwich to prepare for binding. Refer to "Making and Adding Binding" on page 77 and use the remaining deep purple fabric to make 314" of bias binding. Use the binding to finish the edges of the quilt.

4. Don't forget to make a label! Sometimes I like to use leftover fabrics to make another block for the label.

Quilt plan

The
human spirit is
stronger than anything
that can happen to it.
—GEORGE C. SCOTT

Balancing Act

This cheerful quilt balances all the color in the main floral fabric. Step outside your comfort zone and pull together something spectacular with this quick, easy pattern.

Materials

*Yardage is based on fabric that measures 40"
wide after you have prewashed it and trimmed
the selvages.*

- 4 yards of large-scale floral for units,
  squares, flying-geese border units, outer
  border, and binding
- 3 yards of light yellow fabric for units,
  squares, and flying-geese border units
- ¾ yard of dark reddish orange batik for
  units and flying-geese border units
- ½ yard *each* of light green and light
  orange fabric for units and flying-geese
  border units
- ⅜ yard *each* of cocoa brown, turquoise,
  and striped fabric for units and flying-
  geese border units
- 4⅝ yards of fabric for backing
- 81" x 81" piece of batting

CUTTING

*Cut all strips on the crosswise grain (from selvage to selvage)
unless instructed otherwise.*

From the light yellow fabric, cut:

- 14 strips, 3" x 40"; subcut into:
    - 132 squares, 3" x 3"
    - 20 rectangles, 3" x 5½"
- 9 strips, 5½" x 40"; subcut into 57 squares,
  5½" x 5½"
- 2 strips, 3⅜" x 40"; subcut into 20 squares,
  3⅜" x 3⅜". Cut each square once diagonally to
  yield 2 half-square triangles (40 total).

From the light green fabric, cut:

- 4 strips, 3" x 40"; subcut into 24 rectangles, 3" x 5½"

From the light orange fabric, cut:

- 4 strips, 3" x 40"; subcut into 24 rectangles, 3" x 5½"

From the cocoa brown fabric, cut:

- 3 strips, 3" x 40"; subcut into 20 rectangles, 3" x 5½"

From the dark reddish orange batik, cut:

- 3 strips, 3" x 40"; subcut into:
    - 20 squares, 3" x 3"
    - 16 rectangles, 3" x 5½"
- 2 strips, 5⅞" x 40"; subcut into 10 squares, 5⅞" x
  5⅞". Cut each square once diagonally to yield 2 half-
  square triangles (20 total).

From the *lengthwise* grain of the large-scale floral, cut:

- 4 strips, 6" x 80"

From the remaining large-scale floral, cut:

- 24 squares, 5½" x 5½"
- 8 strips, 3" x 40"; subcut into 100 squares, 3" x 3"

From the turquoise fabric, cut:

- 3 strips, 3" x 40"; subcut into 16 rectangles, 3" x 5½"

From the striped fabric, cut:

- 3 strips, 3" x 40"; subcut into 16 rectangles, 3" x 5½"

MAKING THE QUILT

Refer to "Quilting Basics" on page 72 for guidance as
needed. Press seams in the direction indicated by the
arrows.

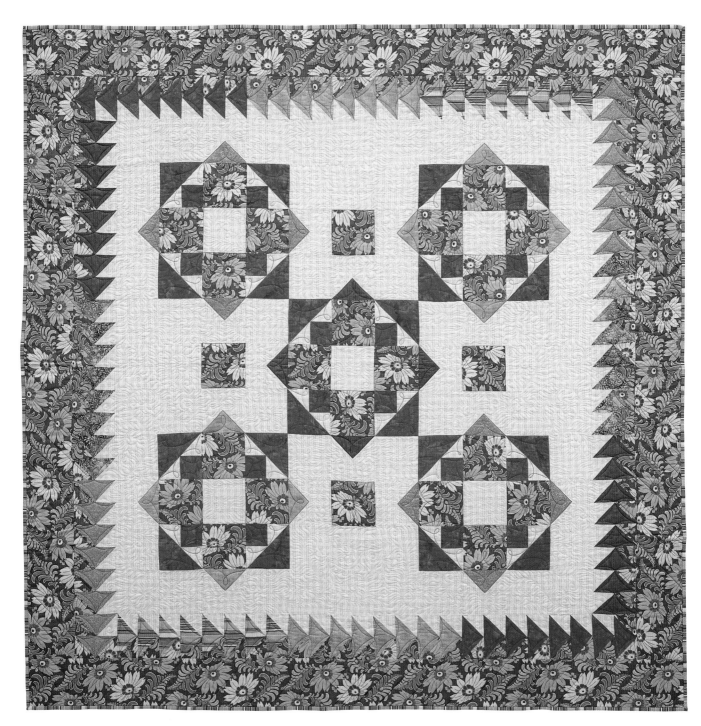

BALANCING ACT

Pieced by Julia Teters-Zeigler. Machine quilted by Kim Stotsenberg.

FINISHED QUILT: 76½" x 76½" • FINISHED UNIT: 5" x 5"

FINISHED FLYING-GEESE UNIT (BORDER): 2½" x 5" • SKILL LEVEL: confident beginner

Making the Units

Although it appears to be made from blocks, this quilt is constructed in rows made from two different pieced units and a series of 5½" squares.

Unit A

1. Mark a diagonal line on the wrong side of each 3" yellow square. Align a marked square right sides together with the left edge of each 3" x 5½" green rectangle and stitch directly on the marked line. Trim ¼" from the stitched line as shown; press. Make eight.

Make 8.

2. Repeat step 1 to stitch a 3" yellow square to the opposite side of the unit as shown. Trim and press. Make eight.

Make 8.

3. Repeat steps 1 and 2 using 3" yellow squares and the 3" x 5½" light orange rectangles. Trim and press. Make eight.

Make 8.

4. Repeat steps 1 and 2 using 3" yellow squares and the 3" x 5½" brown rectangles. Trim and press. Make four.

Make 4.

5. Stitch a 3" x 5½" yellow rectangle to each unit from steps 2–4 as shown; press. Label these unit A.

Unit A

Unit B

1. Stitch a yellow half-square triangle to the right edge of each 3" reddish orange square as shown; press. Make 20.

Make 20.

2. Stitch a remaining yellow half-square triangle to the adjacent (bottom) edge of each unit from step 1 as shown; press. Make 20.

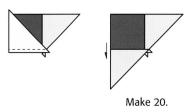

Make 20.

3. Stitch a reddish orange half-square triangle to each unit from step 2 as shown; press. Make 20. Refer to "Squaring Up Blocks" on page 76 and trim the units to 5½" x 5½". Label these unit B.

Unit B.
Make 20.

ASSEMBLING THE QUILT

Arrange units A and B, the 5½" yellow squares, and the 5½" floral squares in 11 horizontal rows, taking care to orient the units as shown. Sew the units and squares into rows; press. Sew the rows together; press. Trim the quilt top to measure 55½" x 55½".

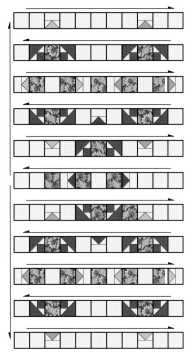

Assembly diagram

ADDING THE BORDERS

Refer to the photo on page 28 as needed.

1. Refer to "Unit A" on page 29. Repeat steps 1 and 2 using one 3" yellow square (left edge), one 3" floral square (right edge), and one 3" x 5½" reddish orange rectangle as shown; press. Make 14. Repeat using two 3" floral squares and one 3" x 5½" reddish orange rectangle as shown. Make two.

Make 14.   Make 2.

2. Repeat step 1 substituting a 3" x 5½" light orange rectangle for the reddish orange rectangle; press.

Make 14.   Make 2.

3. Refer to "Unit A" on page 29. Repeat steps 1 and 2 using one 3" yellow square (left edge), one 3" floral square (right edge), and one 3" x 5½" turquoise rectangle as shown; press. Make 16. Repeat, substituting a 3" x 5½" green rectangle, a 3" x 5½" brown rectangle, or a 3" x 5½" striped rectangle for the turquoise rectangle. Make 16 of each.

Make 16 of each.

4. Refer to the photo on page 28 and the diagrams below. Arrange and sew units from steps 1–3 as shown to make four border units; press. Referring to the photo and diagrams, sew each border unit to the appropriate side of the quilt. Press the seams away from the border.

Top/bottom border.
Make 2.

Side border.
Make 2.

5. Referring to "Mitered Borders" on page 76, sew a 6" x 80" floral outer-border strip to each side of the quilt, mitering the corners. Press the seams toward the outer border.

FINISHING THE QUILT

For detailed instructions on finishing techniques, refer to "Quilting Basics" on page 72.

1. Cut and piece the backing so it is 4" larger than the quilt top. Layer the backing, batting, and quilt top. Baste in preparation for quilting.

2. Hand or machine quilt as desired. The yellow background in the quilt shown is quilted heavily with a light yellow thread in a feathered-vine design. The blocks are quilted with variegated thread in a loop design, and the border is quilted with simple straight lines.

3. Square up the quilt sandwich to prepare for binding. Refer to "Making and Adding Binding" on page 77 and use the remaining floral fabric to make 318" of bias binding. Use the binding to finish the edges of the quilt.

4. Don't forget to make a label! Sometimes I like to use leftover fabrics to make another block for the label.

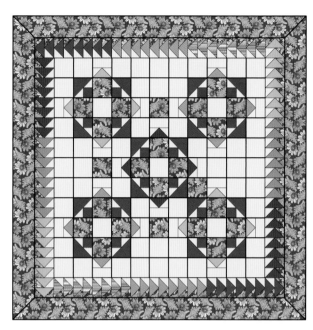

Quilt plan

BODY SPIRIT SOUL MIND BODY

FOUR THINGS THAT every soul needs:

Harmony. The love, clarity, and compassion that emerge within the person who aligns him- or herself with the soul are the same qualities that will bring harmony to other people's lives.

Cooperation. We are together as friends and fellow quilters because we want to be. When we work together, co-creations emerge!

Sharing. Share what is important to you. Give of yourself!

Reverence for life. Reverence is a level of protection and honor about the process of life. While a person is maturing toward the journey and through the journey of authentic empowerment, she or he harms nothing.

Wherever we are, it is but a stage on the way to somewhere else, and whatever we do, however well we do it, it is only a preparation to do something else that shall be different.

—ROBERT LOUIS STEVENSON

Embrace Life

Whimsical, bright polka-dot fabrics dazzle in this darling quilt! The Star blocks are simple and fun to put together. Let your imagination run wild as you choose fabrics from the huge selection of wonderful polka-dot prints that are available.

Materials

Yardage is based on fabric that measures 40" wide after you have prewashed it and trimmed the selvages.

- 1¾ yards of black-and-white polka-dot fabric for framing borders and binding
- 1⅛ yards of striped fabric for outer border
- ¾ yard *each* of 4 assorted white-background polka-dot fabrics for blocks
- ⅝ yard *each* of pink, green, blue, and yellow solids for blocks
- ⅝ yard *each* of 4 assorted black-background polka-dot fabrics for blocks
- ⅜ yard *each* of 4 assorted pink-background polka-dot fabrics for blocks and pieced border
- ⅜ yard *each* of 4 assorted green-background polka-dot fabrics for blocks and pieced border
- ⅜ yard *each* of 4 assorted blue-background polka-dot fabrics for blocks and pieced border
- ⅜ yard *each* of 4 assorted yellow-background polka-dot fabrics for blocks and pieced border
- 7 yards of fabric for backing*
- 84" x 84" piece of batting

This yardage assumes 3 lengths of fabric. If your fabric measures 42" wide after the selvages have been removed and the fabric has been washed, you will need only 4¾ yards (2 lengths).

CUTTING

Cut all strips on the crosswise grain (from selvage to selvage) unless instructed otherwise.

From *each* of the 4 assorted pink-background polka-dot fabrics, cut:

- 4 strips, 2½" x 40" (16 total)

From *each* of the 4 assorted green-background polka-dot fabrics, cut:

- 4 strips, 2½" x 40" (16 total)

From *each* of the 4 assorted blue-background polka-dot fabrics, cut:

- 4 strips, 2½" x 40" (16 total)

From *each* of the 4 assorted yellow-background polka-dot fabrics, cut:

- 4 strips, 2½" x 40" (16 total)

From *each* of the pink, green, blue, and yellow solids, cut:

- 2 strips, 5¾" x 40"; subcut into 8 squares, 5¾" x 5¾" (32 total)

From *each* of the 4 assorted black-background polka-dot fabrics, cut:

- 2 strips, 5¾" x 40"; subcut into 8 squares, 5¾" x 5¾" (32 total)

From *each* of the 4 assorted white-background polka-dot fabrics, cut:

- 2 strips, 4⅞" x 40"; subcut into 16 squares, 4⅞" x 4⅞" (64 total). Cut each square once diagonally to yield 2 half-square triangles (128 total).
- 2 strips, 4½" x 40"; subcut into 16 squares, 4½" x 4½" (64 total)

From the black-and-white polka-dot fabric, cut:

- 16 strips, 1½" x 40"

From the striped fabric, cut:

- 8 strips, 4½" x 40"

MAKING THE QUILT

Refer to "Quilting Basics" on page 72 for guidance as needed. Press seams in the direction indicated by the arrows.

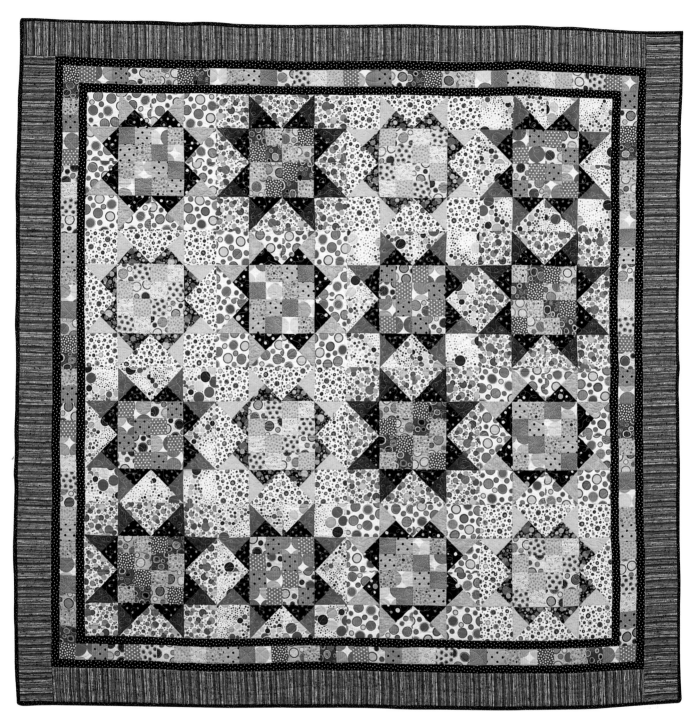

EMBRACE LIFE

Pieced by Monika Harzman. Quilted by Sharon Welsh.

FINISHED QUILT: 80½" x 80½" • FINISHED BLOCK: 16" x 16" • SKILL LEVEL: intermediate

Making the Blocks

You will make 16 blocks for this quilt: 4 identical blocks each in four different colors (pink, green, blue, and yellow). You will pair one black-background polka-dot and one white-background polka-dot fabric with all 4 blocks in each colorway.

1. Assign each of the pink polka-dot fabrics a number from 1 through 4. Arrange four 2½" x 40" strips, one from each pink polka-dot fabric, in the following order: 1-2-3-4. Sew them together to make a strip set as shown; press. Repeat to make three additional strip sets with the strips arranged as follows: 2-3-4-1, 4-1-2-3, and 3-4-1-2. Cut each strip set into four segments, 2½" wide (16 total).

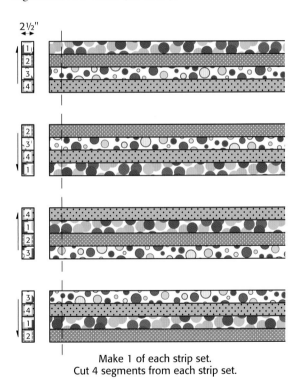

Make 1 of each strip set.
Cut 4 segments from each strip set.

2. Arrange one segment from each strip set as shown and sew together to make a checkerboard unit; press. Make four. Refer to "Squaring Up Blocks" on page 76 and trim the units to 8½" x 8½".

Make 4.

3. Repeat steps 1 and 2 to make four checkerboard units in each color using the 2½" x 40" green, blue, and yellow polka-dot strips.

Make 4 of each.

4. Mark a diagonal line on the wrong side of each 5¾" solid square. Place each marked square right sides together with a 5¾" black-background square. Stitch ¼" from the marked line on both sides as shown. Press well. Use each solid color to make 8 pairings in matching sets of four (32 total). Cut on the marked line. Do not open and press yet.

Make 8
with each color
(32 total).

5. Cut each pair of triangular units from step 4 on the diagonal in the opposite direction from the diagonal seam as shown; press. Make 32 units in each solid color (128 total).

Note: *Half in each color will be mirror-imaged.*

Cut 16 of each pair (128 total).

6. Stitch each unit from step 5 to a white-background half-square triangle as shown. Press the seam open. Make 32 in each solid color in matching sets of 8 (128 total). Again, half in each color will be mirror-imaged. Refer to "Squaring Up Blocks" on page 76 to trim the units to 4½" x 4½".

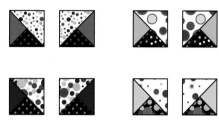

Make 16 of each pair (128 total).

7. Arrange one checkerboard unit from step 2 or 3, four of each matching-colored units from step 6, and four 4½" matching white-background squares as shown. Stitch the units and squares into rows; press. Stitch the rows together; press. Make four identical blocks in each color (16 total).

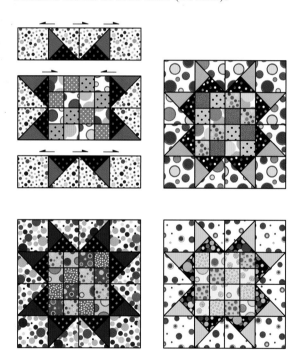

Make 4 of each.

Assembling the Quilt

Following the assembly diagram below, arrange the blocks in four horizontal rows of four blocks each, rotating the blocks as desired for a scrappier look. Sew the blocks into rows; press. Sew the rows together; press. Square up the quilt top to measure 64½" x 64½".

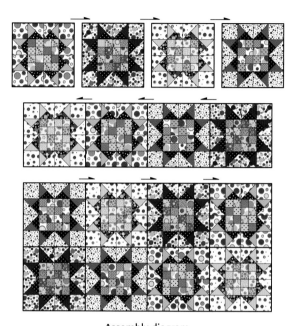

Assembly diagram

Adding the Borders

Refer to the photo on page 34 as needed.

1. Sew two 1½" x 40" black-and-white strips together end to end; press. Make eight. Cut two strips, 1½" x 64½", and two strips, 1½" x 66½", for the first framing border. Cut two strips, 1½" x 70½", and two strips, 1½" x 72½", for the second framing border.

2. Sew the 1½" x 64½" first framing-border strips to the top and bottom of the quilt. Press the seams toward the border. Stitch the 1½" x 66½" first framing-border strips to the sides of the quilt; press.

3. Cut two 2½"-wide polka-dot segments from the leftovers from each strip set on page 35. Cut an additional segment from four of the strip sets. You will have 36 segments total.

4. Stitch nine 2½"-wide polka-dot segments from step 3 together end to end, alternating the colors to make the top pieced border. Remove 3 squares so the unit includes 33 squares; press. Sew to the top of the quilt. Press the seams toward the first framing border. Repeat to make and sew a pieced sashing strip to the bottom of the quilt; press.

5. Repeat step 4 to make two strips with nine segments each for the side borders. Remove 1 square from each so the borders include 35 squares each; press. Sew to the sides of the quilt; press. The quilt should measure 70½" x 70½".

6. Sew the 1½" x 70½" second framing-border strips to the top and bottom of the quilt and the 1½" x 72½" second framing-border strips to the sides. Press the seams toward the second framing border.

7. Sew the 4½" x 40" striped strips together end to end to make one continuous strip. Press the seams to one side. Cut two strips, 4½" x 72½", and two strips, 4½" x 80½".

8. Sew the 4½" x 72½" outer-border strips to the top and bottom of the quilt. Press the seams toward the outer border. Sew the 4½" x 80½" outer-border strips to the sides; press.

FINISHING THE QUILT

For detailed instructions on finishing techniques, refer to "Quilting Basics" on page 72.

1. Cut and piece the backing so it is 4" larger than the quilt top. Layer the backing, batting, and quilt top. Baste in preparation for quilting.

2. Hand or machine quilt as desired. In the quilt shown, the stars are quilted with a loopy meander pattern. The background is quilted in a circle pattern and swirled stars. Simple quilting for such a busy quilt was the perfect solution!

3. Square up the quilt sandwich to prepare for binding. Refer to "Making and Adding Binding" on page 77 and use the remaining black-and-white polka-dot fabric to make 334" of bias binding. Use the binding to finish the edges of the quilt.

4. Don't forget to make a label! Sometimes I like to use leftover fabrics to make another block for the label.

Quilt plan

I HAVE ALWAYS been amazed at how laughter can create so much joy and well-being! Think of a time when you had a great laugh; picture what you were doing and who you were with. It puts a smile on your face right now, doesn't it? Create laughter. Invite several friends over for an "all-nighter" sewing session. Laughter is sure to take over and make the hours fly by! Make a date to work out at the gym with friends who make you laugh. Read an amusing book while soaking in the tub—aah. Rent a funny movie.

Tea Rose Bath Bombs

2 tablespoons citric acid

2 tablespoons cornstarch

¼ cup baking soda

1½ tablespoons almond oil

2 or 3 drops of tea rose essential oil

3 to 4 drops of food coloring (optional)

Mix the citric acid, cornstarch, and baking soda well, making sure there are no lumps. Mix the almond oil, essential oil, and food coloring (if desired) in a separate bowl, and then pour slowly into the dry mix until it is doughy and well-blended. Press into molds or make balls (no larger than golf balls) and leave in a warm, dry place for 24 to 48 hours. Once they're dry, wrap the balls in cellophane. Add to your bath for a fabulous, fizzy soak!

Discover the perfect end to a long, hard day with these fizzy bath bombs. Tea rose essential oil is a wonderful stress reliever.

CREATE JOY

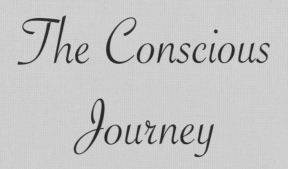

The Conscious
Journey

EACH OF US lives in multiple dimensions. We can choose where to focus our attention, and wherever we focus, a new reality opens up. Through our attention, we bring these dimensions to life. Small changes can be more powerful than big resolutions. One of the things I try to do daily is to keep a journal, writing down my thoughts, dreams, and desires—and sometimes writing just to vent. Writing and repetition are excellent ways to invite deeper thoughts to reveal themselves. An exercise such as journaling allows you to move your attention from the particulars of a problem to an awareness of what you know from a broader perspective. Writing down these thoughts can change your mood and cleanse your soul. Take time—even if it's 10 minutes a day—to focus on just yourself!

One step and then another, and the longest walk is ended. One stitch and then another, and the longest rent is mended. One brick upon another, and the tallest wall is made. One flake and then another, and the deepest snow is laid.

—ANONYMOUS

Navigating the Rapids

Navigating the rapids of daily life can sometimes be daunting. Flow along the path in peace as you stitch this water-themed quilt in rich yet tranquil fabrics. Half-square triangles and square-in-a-square units are simple and piece together rapidly.

Materials

Yardage is based on fabric that measures 40" wide after you have prewashed it and trimmed the selvages.

- 2⅜ yards of a fish print for blocks and outer border
- 1¾ yards of purple print for blocks, inner border, and binding
- 1¼ yards of dark gold print for blocks
- ⅞ yard of light gold print for blocks
- ⅞ yard of olive green print for blocks
- ⅞ yard of red print for blocks and middle border
- 4 yards of fabric for backing
- 70" x 87" piece of batting

Cutting

Cut all strips on the crosswise grain (from selvage to selvage).

From the dark gold print, cut:
- 3 strips, 3⅝" x 40"; subcut into 24 squares, 3⅝" x 3⅝". Cut each square once diagonally to make 2 half-square triangles (48 total).
- 4 strips, 6⅜" x 40"; subcut into 24 squares, 6⅜" x 6⅜"

From the fish print, cut:
- 2 strips, 4⅜" x 40"; subcut into 12 squares, 4⅜" x 4⅜"
- 4 strips, 6⅜" x 40"; subcut into 24 squares, 6⅜" x 6⅜"
- 7 strips, 6" x 40"

From the olive green print, cut:
- 4 strips, 6⅜" x 40"; subcut into 24 squares, 6⅜" x 6⅜"

From the light gold print, cut:
- 4 strips, 6⅜" x 40"; subcut into 24 squares, 6⅜" x 6⅜"

From the red print, cut:
- 4 strips, 3¼" x 40"; subcut into 48 squares, 3¼" x 3¼"
- 8 strips, 1¼" x 40"

From the purple print, cut:
- 3 strips, 2" x 40"; subcut into 48 squares, 2" x 2"
- 8 strips, 2½" x 40"

Making the Quilt

Refer to "Quilting Basics" on page 72 for guidance as needed. Press seams in the direction indicated by the arrows.

Making the Blocks

1. Stitch dark gold half-square triangles to the top and bottom edges of each 4⅜" fish print square; press. Repeat to sew a dark gold half-square triangle to the remaining sides of the unit; press. Make 12. Refer to "Squaring Up Blocks" on page 76 and trim the units to 6" x 6".

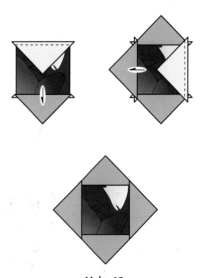

Make 12.

NAVIGATING THE RAPIDS

Pieced and machine quilted by Nancy Workman.

FINISHED QUILT: 66½" x 83" • FINISHED BLOCK: 16½" x 16½" • SKILL LEVEL: confident beginner

2. Mark a diagonal line on the wrong side of each 6⅜" dark gold square. Place each marked square right sides together with a 6⅜" olive green square. Stitch ¼" from the marked line on both sides as shown. Cut on the marked line to make two half-square-triangle units; press. Make 48. Square up each unit to 6" x 6".

Make 48.

3. Repeat step 2 using the light gold squares and the 6⅜" fish print squares. Make 48.

Make 48.

4. Mark a diagonal line on the wrong side of each 3¼" red square. Align a marked square right sides together with the bottom-left corner of each unit from step 3 and stitch directly on the marked line. Trim ¼" from the stitched line as shown; press. Make 48.

Make 48.

5. Repeat step 4 to sew a 2" purple square to each unit from step 4 as shown. Make 48.

Make 48.

6. Arrange one unit from step 1, four units from step 2, and four units from step 5 as shown. Stitch the units together; press. Sew the rows together; press. Make 12.

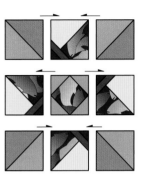 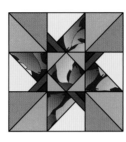

Make 12.

ASSEMBLING THE QUILT

Arrange the blocks in four horizontal rows of three blocks each. Sew the blocks into rows. Press the seams in opposite directions from row to row. Sew the rows together; press. Square up the quilt top to measure 50" x 66½".

ADDING THE BORDERS

Refer to the photo on page 42 as needed.

1. Sew two 2½" x 40" purple strips together end to end and trim to measure 66½" long. Make two and sew to the sides of the quilt. Press the seams toward the border.

2. Sew two 2½" x 40" purple strips together end to end and trim to measure 54" long. Make two and sew to the top and bottom of the quilt; press.

3. Sew two 1¼" x 40" red strips together end to end and trim to measure 70½" long. Make two and sew to the sides of the quilt. Press the seams toward the new border.

4. Sew two 1¼" x 40" red strips together end to end and trim to measure 55½" long. Make two and sew to the top and bottom of the quilt; press.

5. Sew the 6" x 40" fish print strips together end to end to make one continuous strip. Cut two strips, 6" x 72", and sew to the sides of the quilt. Press the seams toward the new border. Cut two strips, 6" x 66½", and sew to the top and bottom of the quilt; press.

Quilt plan

FINISHING THE QUILT

For detailed instructions on finishing techniques, refer to "Quilting Basics" on page 72.

1. Cut and piece the backing so it is 4" larger than the quilt top. Layer the backing (with the seam running horizontally), batting, and quilt top. Baste in preparation for quilting.

2. Hand or machine quilt as desired. Consider a pattern that's subtle to highlight the fabric selection in the quilt. In the quilt shown, the fish fabric top is quilted with an allover wave pattern with fishing lures on the border.

3. Square up the quilt sandwich to prepare for binding. Refer to "Making and Adding Binding" on page 77 and use the remaining purple print to make 311" of bias binding. Use the binding to finish the edges of the quilt.

4. Don't forget to make a label! Sometimes I like to use leftover fabrics to make another block for the label.

Soul Mind BODY Spirit Soul

"PROGRESSIVE RELAXATION" is something you can do while sitting at your sewing machine—after you've taken out a seam for the zillionth time!

Close your eyes and place your feet on the ground and your hands on your knees. Take 10 very calculated and even breaths in and out. Start the relaxation with your toes: tighten them up as hard as you can, and then consciously feel them as you let go, loosen, and allow them to go limp. Do this with your legs, arms, hands, tummy, and bottom. Don't forget your shoulders and neck; feel how heavy they can be, and will them to relax and go limp. Continue breathing evenly as you go through these steps. The objective is to feel every part of your body relax!

BREATHE

Pieced by Julia Teters-Zeigler, 66½" x 83". Machine quilted by Karen Snyder.

This scrappy blue and green alternate version of "Navigating the Rapids" is quilted in an allover swirl pattern.

A journey of
a thousand miles
must begin with
a single step.
—CHINESE PROVERB

Pathfinder

Resolve to be your best as you walk along this path. This table topper combines three simple techniques in a fast and easy project.

Materials

Yardage is based on fabric that measures 40" wide after you have prewashed it and trimmed the selvages.

- 1¾ yards of large-scale floral for sashing, outer border, and binding
- ¾ yard of red solid for blocks and middle flat-piping border
- ⅝ yard of dark turquoise print for blocks and inner flat-piping border
- ½ yard of tan print for blocks
- ¼ yard of yellowish gold print for blocks
- 1 fat quarter of blue-and-gold cotton lamé for blocks*
- 1 fat quarter of red-and-gold cotton lamé for blocks*
- 1¼ yards of fabric for backing
- 41" x 41" piece of batting

Lamé is a fabric with metallic threads woven into the design. Cotton lamés can be found at your local quilt shop. Please note that they fray easily, so handle gently.

CUTTING

Cut all strips on the crosswise grain (from selvage to selvage).

From the tan print, cut:

- 2 strips, 2⅞" x 40"; subcut into 16 squares, 2⅞" x 2⅞"
- 2 strips, 2½" x 40"; subcut into 20 squares, 2½" x 2½"
- 2 strips, 1½" x 40"; subcut into 32 squares, 1½" x 1½"

From the red solid, cut:

- 1 strip, 2⅞" x 40"; subcut into 8 squares, 2⅞" x 2⅞"
- 2 strips, 1½" x 40"; subcut into:
    - 8 squares, 1½" x 1½"
    - 16 rectangles, 1½" x 2½"
- 1 strip, 2½" x 40"; subcut into 8 squares, 2½" x 2½"
- 4 strips, 2½" x 40"

From the dark turquoise print, cut:

- 1 strip, 2⅞" x 40"; subcut into 8 squares, 2⅞" x 2⅞"
- 2 strips, 1½" x 40"; subcut into:
    - 8 squares, 1½" x 1½"
    - 16 rectangles, 1½" x 2½"
- 1 strip, 2½" x 40"; subcut into 8 squares, 2½" x 2½"
- 4 strips, 1½" x 40"

From the yellowish gold print, cut:

- 2 strips, 1½" x 40"; subcut into 32 squares, 1½" x 1½"
- 1 square, 2½" x 2½"

From the blue-and-gold cotton lamé, cut:

- 3 strips, 2½" x 20"; subcut into 8 squares, 2½" x 2½"

From the red-and-gold cotton lamé, cut:

- 3 strips, 2½" x 20"; subcut into 8 squares, 2½" x 2½"

From the large-scale floral, cut:

- 4 strips, 2½" x 10½"
- 2 strips, 2½" x 22½"
- 2 strips, 2½" x 26½"
- 4 strips, 6" x 40"

MAKING THE QUILT

Refer to "Quilting Basics" on page 72 for guidance as needed. Press seams in the direction indicated by the arrows.

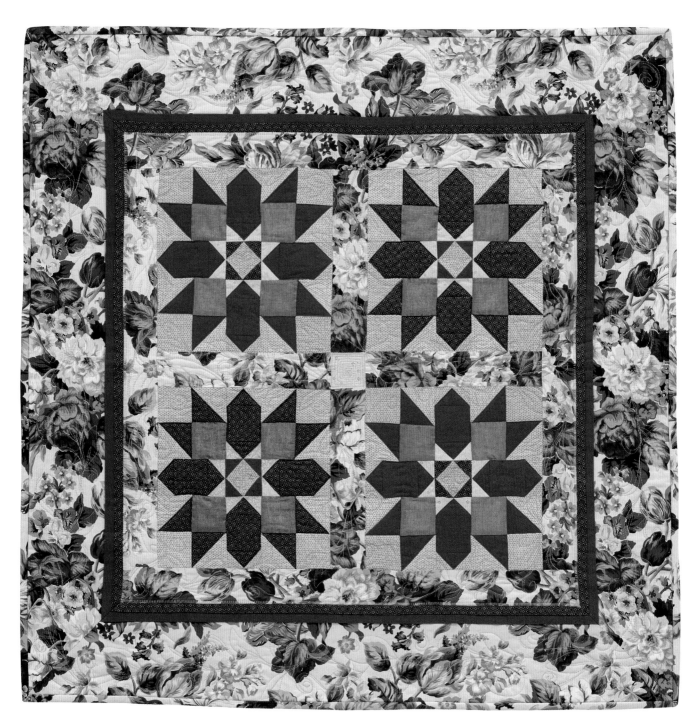

PATHFINDER

Pieced and machine quilted by Julia Teters-Zeigler,

in loving memory of her dear father-in-law, Jack E. Zeigler Sr.

FINISHED QUILT: 37½" x 37½" • FINISHED BLOCK: 10" x 10" • SKILL LEVEL: intermediate

Making the Blocks

1. Mark a diagonal line on the wrong side of 32 tan 2⅞" squares. Place each marked square right sides together with a 2⅞" red solid or 2⅞" turquoise square. Stitch ¼" from the marked line on both sides as shown. Cut on the marked line to make two half-square-triangle units; press. Make 16 of each. Square up each unit to 2½" x 2½".

Make 16 of each.

2. Mark a diagonal line on the wrong side of each 1½" red solid square. Align a marked square right sides together with the upper-right and lower-left corners of one 2½" tan square and stitch directly on the marked line. Trim ¼" from the stitched line as shown; press. Repeat to stitch a 1½" red square to the upper-left and lower-right corners of each unit as shown. Trim and press. Make two.

Make 2.

3. Repeat step 2 using the 1½" turquoise squares and 2½" tan squares. Make two.

Make 2.

4. Mark a diagonal line on the wrong side of each 1½" tan square. Align a marked square right sides together with the left edge of each 1½" x 2½" turquoise rectangle and stitch directly on the marked line. Trim ¼" from the stitched line as shown; press. Make eight.

Make 8.

5. Repeat step 4 to stitch a 1½" tan square to the opposite side of the unit as shown. Trim and press. Make eight.

Make 8.

6. Repeat steps 4 and 5 using the 1½" yellowish gold squares and 1½" x 2½" turquoise rectangles. Make eight.

Make 8.

7. Repeat steps 4 and 5 using the 1½" tan squares and 1½" x 2½" red rectangles. Make eight.

Make 8.

8. Repeat steps 4 and 5 using the 1½" yellowish gold squares and 1½" x 2½" red rectangles. Make eight.

Make 8.

9. Stitch one 2½" turquoise square between a unit from step 5 and a unit from step 6 as shown; press. Make eight.

Make 8.

10. Repeat step 9 using one 2½" red square and one unit each from steps 7 and 8. Make eight.

Make 8.

11. Arrange one 2½" tan square, one 2½" blue cotton lamé square, and two turquoise/tan units from step 1 as shown. Stitch the units and squares into rows; press. Sew the rows together; press. Make eight.

Make 8.

12. Repeat step 11 using one 2½" tan square, one 2½" red cotton lamé square, and two red/tan units from step 1. Make eight.

Make 8.

13. Arrange one unit from step 2, four units from step 9, and four units from step 11 as shown. Stitch the units into rows; press. Sew the rows together; press. Make two. Repeat using one unit from step 3, four units from step 10, and four units from step 12. Make two. Refer to "Squaring Up Blocks" on page 76 and trim each block to 10½" x 10½".

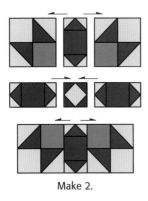

Make 2.

Make 2.

ASSEMBLING THE QUILT

1. Sew one 2½" x 10½" floral sashing strip between two blocks, one of each color, as shown; press. Make two.

Make 2.

2. Sew the 2½" yellowish gold square between two 2½" x 10½" floral sashing strips; press.

3. Following the assembly diagram below, sew the unit from step 2 between the two units from step 1; press.

4. Pin and stitch the 2½" x 22½" floral sashing strips to the sides of the unit; press. Pin and stitch the 2½" x 26½" floral sashing strips to the top and bottom; press.

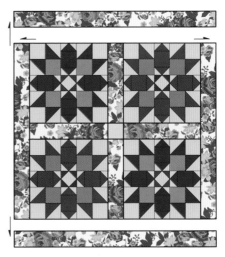

Assembly diagram

ADDING THE BORDERS

Refer to the photo on page 48 as needed.

1. Press each 1½" x 40" turquoise strip in half lengthwise with wrong sides together to create a flat-piping strip. Repeat with each 2½" x 40" red solid strip. Make four of each.

2. Refer to "Mitered Borders" on page 76. With right sides together and raw edges aligned, layer the quilt top, one turquoise flat-piping strip, one red solid flat-piping strip, and one 6" x 40" floral border strip. Pin and stitch. Press the seams toward the border. Repeat to sew a turquoise flat-piping strip, a red flat-piping strip, and a floral border strip to each remaining side of the quilt, mitering the corners; press.

Finishing the Quilt

For detailed instructions on finishing techniques, refer to "Quilting Basics" on page 72.

1. Cut and piece the backing so it is 4" larger than the quilt top. Layer the backing, batting, and quilt top. Baste in preparation for quilting.

2. Hand or machine quilt as desired. In the quilt shown, each star is quilted in the ditch, and the rest of the quilt is quilted with gold thread in a gentle leaf-and-swirl pattern.

3. Square up the quilt sandwich to prepare for binding. Refer to "Making and Adding Binding" on page 77 and use the remaining floral print to make 160" of bias binding. Use the binding to finish the edges of the quilt.

4. Don't forget to make a label! Sometimes I like to use leftover fabrics to make another block for the label.

Quilt plan

M AKE DECISIONS FROM well-founded convictions. All thoughtless acts and meaningless doings should be kept distant from your soul. Be steadfast in your convictions! Make it one of your convictions to take a few minutes every day to quilt, to think about future projects, or simply to peruse a beloved quilt book. Stay steadfast in your passion!

Buckwheat Eye Mask

Cut two pieces of fabric, 6" x 11". With right sides together, stitch ¼" from the raw edges. Leave a 2½" opening at one end. Clip the corners and turn the mask right side out. Fill with 2½ cups of buckwheat (you can also use rice) and stitch the opening closed by hand. Embellish as desired. You might want to add lavender or rose petals.

Heat in the microwave for a warm, soothing mask, or chill in the freezer for a cool, refreshing mask!

This mask will be your own private oasis of serenity and comfort. Warm or cold,
place gently over your eyes for a refreshing "mini vacation," if only for a few minutes.

CONVICTION

When
we accept tough
jobs as a challenge
and wade into them
with joy and enthusiasm,
miracles can happen.
—ARLAND GILBERT

Road to Riches

Three basic shapes—a triangle, a trapezoid, and a parallelogram—make up this star-studded quilt. It may sound a little tricky, but it's not! Once you've cut out the pieces, the sewing goes rather quickly. Accept the challenge and watch your miracle evolve.

ROAD TO RICHES

Pieced by Julia Teters-Zeigler. Machine quilted by Jeri Lindstrom.

FINISHED QUILT: 61½" x 68½" • FINISHED BLOCK: 7½" on each side • SKILL LEVEL: advanced

Cutting

Cut all strips on the crosswise grain (from selvage to selvage) unless instructed otherwise. Patterns appear on page 58. Refer to "Making and Using Templates" on page 73 as needed.

From *each* of the 4 assorted tan prints, cut:
- 78 A pieces (312 total)
- 26 B pieces (104 total)

From 2 of the tan prints, cut:
- 20 C pieces (40 total)

From the remaining 2 tan prints, cut:
- 19 C pieces (38 total)

From the red print, cut:
- 117 C pieces
- 10 strips, 1½" x 40"; subcut 2 of the strips into 8 strips, 1½" x 7½"

From the blue print, cut:
- 117 C pieces
- 4 squares, 1½" x 1½"

From the *lengthwise* grain of the cheddar gold print, cut:
- 2 strips, 7½" x 52½"
- 2 strips, 7½" x 45½"
- 4 squares, 7½" x 7½"

Making the Quilt

Refer to "Quilting Basics" on page 72 for guidance as needed. Press seams in the direction indicated by the arrows.

Making the Blocks

1. Stitch a tan A piece to a tan B piece as shown. Press the seam open.

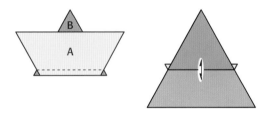

2. Stitch a red C piece to the right end of a tan A piece as shown. Press the seam open.

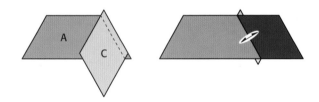

3. Stitch red C pieces to opposite ends of a tan A piece as shown. Press the seams open.

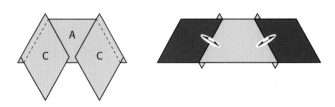

4. Stitch one unit from step 2 and one unit from step 3 to the unit from step 1. Press the seams open to eliminate bulk.

5. Repeat steps 1–4 to make 27 units with all red C pieces, 27 units with all blue C pieces, 11 units with one tan C piece and two red C pieces, 11 units with one tan C piece and two blue C pieces, 14 units with one red C piece and two tan C pieces, and 14 units with one blue C piece and two tan C pieces as shown.

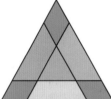

Make 27 of each.

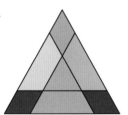
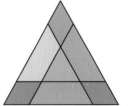

Make 11 of each.

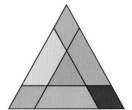
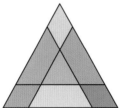

Make 14 of each.

ASSEMBLING THE QUILT

1. Following the assembly diagram below, arrange the units in eight horizontal rows of 13 units each, taking care to place the different-colored units as shown. Sew the units together into rows. Press the seams open. Sew the rows together. Press the seams open.

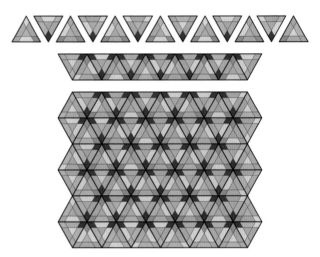

Assembly diagram

2. Use a rotary cutter and rotary ruler to trim the right and left edges of the quilt top as shown. Be sure to leave a ¼" seam allowance on each side. The quilt should now measure 45½" x 52½".

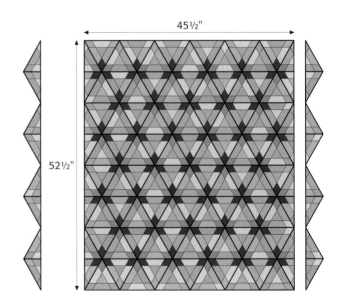

45½"

52½"

Adding the Borders

Refer to the photo on page 54 as needed.

1. Sew two red 1½" x 40" inner-border strips together end to end; press. Make four. Trim two strips to measure 1½" x 52½" and two to measure 1½" x 45½".

2. Sew the 1½" x 52½" red inner-border strips to the 7½" x 52½" cheddar outer-border strips; press. Make two and sew them to the sides of the quilt. Press the seams toward the outer border.

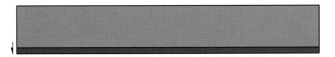

Make 2.

3. Sew the 1½" x 45½" red inner-border strips to the 7½" x 45½" cheddar outer-border strips; press. Make two.

4. Stitch a 1½" x 7½" red strip to a 7½" cheddar square; press. Stitch a 1½" blue square to a 1½" x 7½" red strip; press. Stitch the units together as shown; press. Make four.

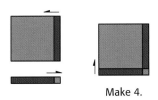

Make 4.

5. Stitch units from step 4 to opposite ends of a pieced border unit from step 3. Press the seams toward the border unit. Make two. Sew to the top and bottom of the quilt; press.

Make 2.

Finishing the Quilt

For detailed instructions on finishing techniques, refer to "Quilting Basics" on page 72.

1. Cut and piece the backing so it is 4" larger than the quilt top. Layer the backing, batting, and quilt top. Baste in preparation for quilting.

2. Hand or machine quilt as desired. The quilt shown was quilted in a variety of Japanese-themed motifs.

3. Square up the quilt sandwich to prepare for binding. Refer to "Making and Adding Binding" on page 77 and use the remaining cheddar fabric to make 270" of bias binding. Use the binding to finish the edges of the quilt.

4. Don't forget to make a label! Sometimes I like to use leftover fabrics to make another block for the label.

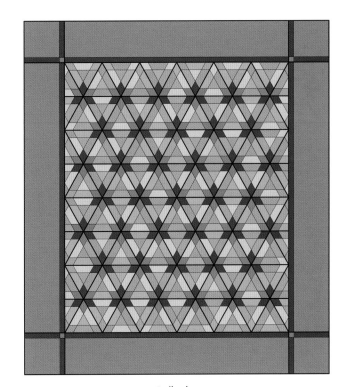

Quilt plan

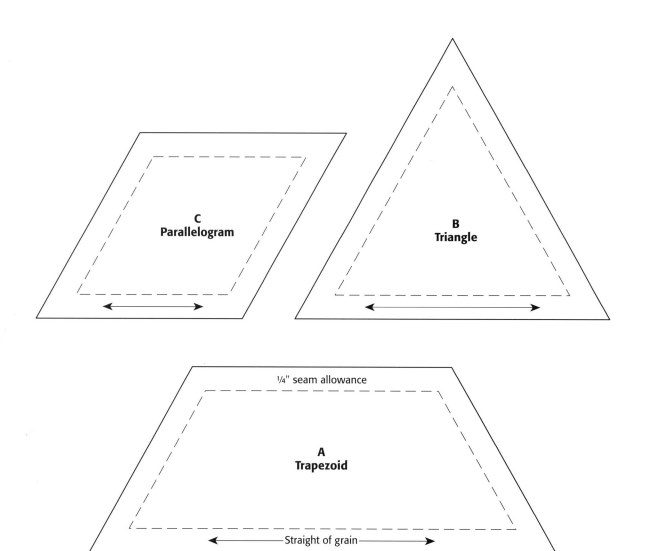

C
Parallelogram

B
Triangle

¼" seam allowance

A
Trapezoid

Straight of grain

Living in the Light

As you walk along the path of self-awareness, consider your senses, the five essential senses that we all have. When was the last time you were really aware of them?

Sight. Strive to learn as much as possible from everything you do. Nothing happens that does not provide an opportunity to gain experiences that are useful in life. You can learn from every person when you choose to pay attention.

Hearing. A person who strives for higher achievement speaks with sense and meaning. Talk for the sake of talk, idle chitchat, and gossip can be harmful. It is so easy to slip into talking about others, but what is the benefit from this? Is it taking up precious time you could be using for something meaningful?

Instead of talking, try to listen! You will be amazed at how much more you hear. Carefully consider the words you do use. Think about your own feelings and how it would affect you if someone were saying your exact words to you! Learn the difference between truth and opinion. So often we judge before we know all the facts. If you listen to others with your heart, remain still inside, and set aside all opinion, you will find a special peace within.

Smell. Do you ever smell something—sometimes ever so faintly—that brings a special memory to mind? Bask in the moment of that memory. My grandmother wore a certain perfume for as many years as I can remember. Every now and then I will catch a whiff of that scent. Sometimes it brings tears to my eyes, but most of the time it brings a smile. I can close my eyes at that moment and feel her patting my hand in her gentle way and saying, "Julie dear . . ." She was such a gracious woman; I hope the scent of her perfume will always make me stop and remember what she meant to our whole family.

Taste. Eating—how many among us can say we don't like to eat? Whether you cook or go out, when was the last time you really savored every bite? For many of us, chocolate is something we can't live without. To me, chocolate is like fabric: I can't imagine a day without it!

Touch. Fabric, fabric, fabric. Sometimes when I can't decide which project to work on, or I need a new idea to rejuvenate myself, I'll sit down in my sewing room with my stash of fabric. Enjoy the feel of the fabrics—soft fuzzy flannels, buttery-soft cottons—you'd be amazed at how inspired you can become just by focusing on the feel of the fabric. It's almost as if the fabrics are calling out to you for a certain project!

Vision of the Future

Learning something new can be exciting, and this quilt offers the perfect opportunity to learn machine appliqué. The appliqué adds a soft curve to your blocks as the stars swirl around the floral background.

Materials

Yardage is based on fabric that measures 40" wide after you have prewashed it and trimmed the selvages.

- 5 yards of large-scale floral for setting pieces and border
- 2 yards of dark green print for block frames and binding
- 1⅜ yards of light melon print for blocks and appliqués
- 1⅜ yards of light green print for blocks and appliqués
- 1¼ yards of cream tone-on-tone print for blocks
- ¼ yard of dark melon print for appliqués
- 8 yards of fabric for backing
- 96" x 96" piece of batting
- Small piece of template material

CUTTING

Cut all strips on the crosswise grain (from selvage to selvage) unless instructed otherwise. Appliqué pattern appears on page 65. Refer to "Appliqué" on page 74 as needed.

From the cream tone-on-tone print, cut:
- 4 strips, 4⅞" x 40"; subcut into 32 squares, 4⅞" x 4⅞"
- 4 strips, 4½" x 40"; subcut into 32 squares, 4½" x 4½"

From the light green print, cut:
- 4 strips, 4⅞" x 40"; subcut into 32 squares, 4⅞" x 4⅞"
- 32 ellipse appliqués

From the light melon print, cut:
- 4 strips, 4⅞" x 40"; subcut into 32 squares, 4⅞" x 4⅞"
- 32 ellipse appliqués

From the dark green print, cut:
- 2 strips, 2½" x 32½"
- 4 strips, 2½" x 40"
- 4 strips, 2½" x 16½"
- 8 strips, 2½" x 18½"

From the *lengthwise* grain of the large-scale floral, cut:
- 4 strips, 10" x 96"

From the remaining large-scale floral, cut:
- 4 strips, 18½" x 32½"

From the dark melon print, cut:
- 16 ellipse appliqués

MAKING THE QUILT

Refer to "Quilting Basics" on page 72 for guidance as needed. Press seams in the direction indicated by the arrows.

MAKING THE BLOCKS

1. Mark a diagonal line on the wrong side of each 4⅞" cream square. Place each marked square right sides together with a 4⅞" light green square or a 4⅞" light melon square. Stitch ¼" from the marked line on both sides as shown. Cut on the marked line to make two half-square-triangle units. Press the seams open to reduce the bulk. Make 32 of each. Refer to "Squaring Up Blocks" on page 76 and trim the units to 4½" x 4½".

Make 32 of each.

VISION OF THE FUTURE
Pieced by Shirlene Gore and Julia Teters-Zeigler.
Appliquéd by Julia Teters-Zeigler. Machine quilted by Patti Bochey.
FINISHED QUILT: 91½" x 91½" • FINISHED BLOCK: 16" x 16" • SKILL LEVEL: confident beginner

2. Repeat step 1 using the remaining 4⅞" light green and light melon squares. Make 32.

Make 32.

3. Arrange four light green and four light melon units from step 1, four units from step 2, and four 4½" cream squares as shown. Stitch the units and squares into rows. Press the seams open. Sew the rows together; press. Make eight.

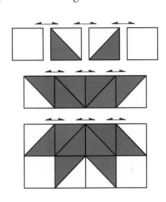

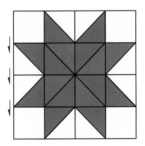

Make 8.

4. Refer to "Appliqué" on page 74 and use your favorite method to appliqué four light melon ellipse appliqués and four light green ellipse appliqués to each block as shown.

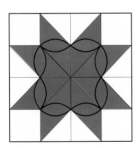

ASSEMBLING THE QUILT

1. Arrange four blocks as shown. Sew the blocks together into rows. Press the seams open. Sew the rows together. Press the seams open.

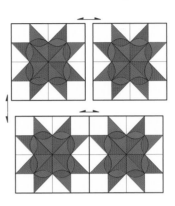

2. Referring to the diagram below as needed, stitch the 2½" x 32½" dark green strips to the top and bottom of the unit from step 1. Press the seams toward the strips.

3. Referring to the diagram, stitch an 18½" x 32½" floral strip to the top and bottom of the unit from step 2 as shown; press.

4. Sew two 2½" x 40" dark green strips together end to end. Press the seams in one direction. Make two. Cut two strips, 2½" x 72½", and stitch them to the sides of the unit from step 3 as shown; press.

5. Stitch a 2½" x 16½" dark green strip to one side of each remaining block as shown; press. Stitch a 2½" x 18½" dark green strip to the top and bottom; press. Make four.

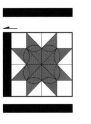

Make 4.

6. Stitch a unit from step 5 to the top and bottom of each remaining 18½" x 32½" floral strip as shown; press. Make two.

Make 2.

7. Stitch the units from step 6 to opposite sides of the unit from step 4; press.

Assembly diagram

8. Referring to the photo on page 62, the diagram below, and "Appliqué" on page 74, use your favorite method to appliqué four dark melon ellipse appliqués to each intersection of the center panel as shown.

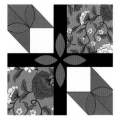

ADDING THE BORDER

Refer to the photo on page 62 as needed. Referring to "Mitered Borders" on page 76, sew a 10" x 96" floral strip to each side of the quilt, mitering the corners. Press the seams toward the border.

FINISHING THE QUILT

For detailed instructions on finishing techniques, refer to "Quilting Basics" on page 72.

1. Cut and piece the backing so it is 4" larger than the quilt top. Layer the backing, batting, and quilt top. Baste in preparation for quilting.

2. Hand or machine quilt as desired. In the quilt shown, the cream background areas are quilted with cream-colored thread in a Celtic heart pattern. The center of each star is quilted with variegated thread in a medallion pattern, and the rest of the quilt is quilted with gentle floral swirls.

3. Square up the quilt sandwich to prepare for binding. Refer to "Making and Adding Binding" on page 77 and use the remaining dark green fabric to make 382" of bias binding. Use the binding to finish the edges of the quilt.

4. Don't forget to make a label! Sometimes I like to use leftover fabrics to make another block for the label.

Quilt plan

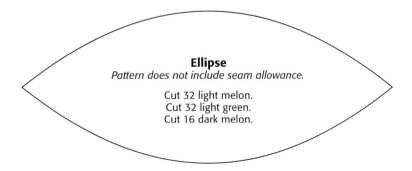

Ellipse
Pattern does not include seam allowance.

Cut 32 light melon.
Cut 32 light green.
Cut 16 dark melon.

IN EVERYTHING YOU do, consider your senses. See, hear, touch, smell, and taste! Allow yourself the time each day to appreciate every sense.

Lavender oil is widely used in aromatherapy to ease tension, tiredness, or anxiety.
Sweet custom labels and beribboned bottles make a charming presentation.

ALLOW YOURSELF TIME

Spirit Mind BODY Spirit Soul

JUST A FEW drops of this lavender bath oil in a hot bath will relieve the tensions of your day and produce a pleasant drowsiness. In a cool bath, it will refresh and energize!

Lavender Bath Oil

3 tablespoons olive oil

6 tablespoons almond oil

3 tablespoons sesame oil

2 tablespoons canola oil

2 tablespoons wheat germ oil

15 to 30 drops lavender essential oil

Mix all the ingredients and shake well. Pour into pretty 1-ounce bottles and add 1 to 2 teaspoons to your bath.

We
have only this
moment, sparkling like
a star in our hand . . .
and melting like a snowflake.
Let us use it before
it is too late.
—MARIE BEYNON RAY

Evolution

I love to relax with a wonderful piece of hand appliqué, and this is a great project to take on the go!
Find a few minutes here and there to appliqué, and before you know it the quilt is ready to assemble.
This simple appliqué creates a gentle circular motion when combined with the fast, easy-to-piece blocks.

EVOLUTION

Pieced and hand appliquéd by Linda Jackson. Quilted by Jeri Lindstrom.

FINISHED QUILT: 52½" x 64½" • FINISHED BLOCK: 12" x 12" • SKILL LEVEL: intermediate

Materials

Yardage is based on fabric that measures 40" wide after you have prewashed it and trimmed the selvages.

- 3 yards of large-scale floral for blocks and outer border
- 1⅞ yards of plum small-scale floral for appliqué and binding
- 1⅝ yards of apricot solid for blocks and inner border
- ⅝ yard of plum solid for blocks
- 3⅛ yards of fabric for backing
- 56" x 68" piece of batting
- Sheet of template material

CUTTING

Cut all strips on the crosswise grain (from selvage to selvage) unless instructed otherwise. Appliqué pattern appears on page 71. Refer to "Appliqué" on page 74 as needed.

From the *lengthwise* grain of the apricot solid, cut:
- 2 strips, 2½" x 48½"
- 2 strips, 2½" x 40½"

From the remaining apricot solid, cut:
- 48 squares, 3½" x 3½"
- 48 squares, 1½" x 1½"

From the plum solid, cut:
- 5 strips, 3½" x 40; subcut into 48 squares, 3½" x 3½"

From the *lengthwise* grain of the large-scale floral, cut:
- 4 strips, 6½" x 52½"

From the remaining large-scale floral, cut:
- 48 squares, 6½" x 6½"

From the plum small-scale floral, cut:
- 48 petal appliqués

MAKING THE QUILT

Refer to "Quilting Basics" on page 72 for guidance as needed. Press seams in the direction indicated by the arrows.

MAKING THE BLOCKS

1. Mark a diagonal line on the wrong side of each 3½" apricot square and each 3½" plum square. Align a marked apricot square right sides together with the upper-right corner of one 6½" large-scale floral square and stitch directly on the marked line. Trim ¼" from the stitched line as shown. Press the seam open. Repeat to sew a 3½" plum square to the lower-left corner of each unit as shown. Trim and press. Make 48.

Make 48.

2. Repeat step 1 to stitch a 1½" apricot square to the bottom-left corner of each unit from step 1. Make 48.

Make 48.

3. Arrange four units from step 2, taking care to turn the units as shown. Stitch the units into rows; press. Sew the rows together; press. Make 12. Refer to "Squaring Up Blocks" on page 76 and trim the blocks to 12½" x 12½".

Make 12.

4. Refer to "Appliqué" on page 74 and use your favorite method to appliqué four petal appliqués so they meet in the center of each block as shown.

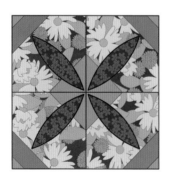

ASSEMBLING THE QUILT

Following the assembly diagram below, arrange the blocks in four horizontal rows of three blocks each. Sew the blocks into rows; press. Sew the rows together; press.

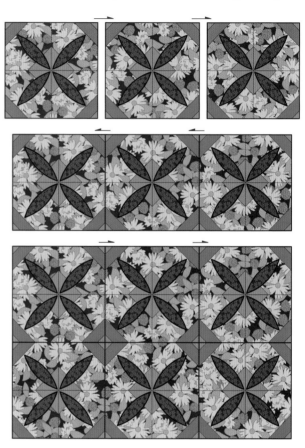

Assembly diagram

ADDING THE BORDERS

Refer to the photo on page 68 as needed.

1. Sew the 2½" x 48½" apricot inner-border strips to the sides of the quilt. Press the seams toward the border. Sew the 2½" x 40½" apricot inner-border strips to the top and bottom; press.

2. Sew 6½" x 52½" large-scale floral outer-border strips to the sides of the quilt. Press the seams toward the outer border. Sew 6½" x 52½" floral outer-border strips to the top and bottom; press.

Quilt plan

FINISHING THE QUILT

For detailed instructions on finishing techniques, refer to "Quilting Basics" on page 72.

1. Cut and piece the backing so it is 4" larger than the quilt top. Layer the backing (with the seam running horizontally), batting, and quilt top. Baste in preparation for quilting.

2. Hand or machine quilt as desired. The quilt shown is quilted in a subtle geometric pattern that enhances the beauty of the appliqué. The borders are quilted with a flowing swirl-and-leaf pattern.

3. Square up the quilt sandwich to prepare for binding. Refer to "Making and Adding Binding" on page 77 and use the remaining plum print fabric to make 246" of bias binding. Use the binding to finish the edges of the quilt.

4. Don't forget to make a label! Sometimes I like to use leftover fabrics to make another block for the label.

BODY SOUL MIND

Be at peace with your quilting and embrace every moment you have to create a legacy for generations to come.

EMBRACE

Petal
Pattern does not include seam allowance.

Cut 48.

QUILTING BASICS

READ THROUGH THESE basic instructions before beginning any project. Should you want more detailed information about any of the steps, you'll find many wonderful books available as resources. The most important thing about quilting is that it is *your* experience, so find a method that you are most comfortable with. Every teacher has his or her own "right" way, but it isn't right for you unless you're comfortable with it. This is the ultimate creative experience—wander, enjoy, and try something new!

> To grow and know what one is growing towards—that is the source of all strength and confidence in life.
> —JAMES BAILLIE

FABRIC AND THREAD

I recommend that you use 100%-cotton fabric, which is the most durable for quilting. I also recommend that you prewash and press all yardage before you cut it into pieces. This will save you the headache of possible bleeding, crocking, or shrinkage in your finished quilt.

Fabric typically comes 44" to 45" wide on the bolt. Once you have laundered the fabric and trimmed off the selvage, you'll have approximately 42" of usable width. Yardage amounts and cutting instructions in this book are based on 40" of usable fabric to allow for any variation.

When you use 100%-cotton fabric, use 100%-cotton thread. In my experience, the durability of the quilt increases when I use good-quality cotton thread for piecing cotton fabrics. Every quilter has an opinion about this, however, so feel free to experiment.

A NOTE TO ALL BEGINNERS

WE WERE ALL beginners at one time, and we all learned the same way you are now, one step at a time. Feel free to ask for help from your local quilt shop. Most shops are more than happy to talk you through each step and recommend books that may be helpful. The only thing that you, as a beginning quilter, should remember is that the only stupid question is the one you do not ask.

TOOLS

The following general tools are helpful for making the quilts in this book.

Rotary cutter and self-healing mat. A rotary cutter is a cutting tool that features a round, sharp blade that can cut through several layers of fabric at one time. Any brand is fine; find one that you feel comfortable with. Rotary cutters come in several sizes; the medium size is a good one to start with.

Always use a self-healing mat when you use your rotary cutter. Mat boards come in several sizes. You may want to start with a medium-sized mat and add other sizes later if you feel the need for them.

Acrylic ruler. Use this sturdy, thick, clear plastic ruler for making straight cuts with a rotary cutter. Many sizes and brands of ruler are available. Choose one with easy-to-read markings.

Scissors. You'll need one pair of good-quality scissors for cutting fabric only, a utility pair for cutting paper or template material, and one small pair of sharp, quality scissors for clipping threads.

Keep your scissors for cutting fabric and thread in a place where family members will not be tempted to borrow them for other uses. Using them to cut paper, cardboard, or other materials will damage your sewing scissors, and they will not be as effective when cutting fabric or thread.

Template material. Quilters use many materials for making templates, including template plastic, cardboard, sandpaper, and freezer paper. I prefer template plastic and freezer paper, because I can see through them to trace the pattern.

If you're planning to hand quilt, you'll need the following tools also.

Frame or hoop. You'll get smaller, tighter stitches if you stretch your quilt for quilting. A frame supports the quilt's weight and ensures the tension with each stitch. Quilting hoops are portable and sturdier than embroidery hoops and can handle the thickness of the quilt layers.

Quilting needles. A quilting or Between needle is a short needle with a small eye. Common sizes are 8, 9, and 10; the higher numbers indicate the smaller needles. Size 8 is best for beginners.

Quilting thread. Choose a 100%-cotton hand-quilting thread. The thread can match or contrast with the fabric, depending upon your preference.

Thimble. There are thimbles available in several materials, styles, and sizes. Find one that you feel most comfortable with. I use a leather thimble that conforms to the shape of my finger.

For machine quilting, you will need the following supplies.

Walking foot. This foot walks along the layers of the quilt, feeding them evenly and without the pulling that can create puckers on the back of your quilt. Use it for quilting straight lines, commonly known as "stitching in the ditch" (stitching between the seams) of your pieced quilt top.

Darning foot. Sometimes called a hopper foot, this attachment is used for free-motion stitching (stitching in any direction with the feed dogs down). You may find that your machine has this attachment in the accessory kit. If not, bring the name of the model and make of your machine when you purchase a darning foot to fit.

Quilting thread. Use 100%-cotton thread for both your bobbin and your top thread. If you choose to use clear or "smoke" nylon thread on the quilt top, use a cotton thread in the bobbin.

MAKING AND USING TEMPLATES

To make a template, place the template material on the printed pattern page and use a laundry marker or permanent fine-tip marking pen to trace each pattern piece.

Place the template on the right side of the appropriate fabric and use the marking tool of your choice to trace around the template. (I use a pencil or chalk.) Pay close attention to the pattern to see if it includes a ¼" seam allowance. Patterns for piecing (for example, "Road to Riches" on page 53) include a ¼" seam allowance. Patterns for appliqué do not. To add a ¼" seam allowance to appliqué pieces, cut out the fabric shape ¼" beyond the traced line.

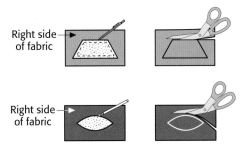

PIECING THE QUILT

Machine piecing requires sewing an exact ¼" seam. Some machines have a presser foot that is ¼" wide, or they have a special attachment available. (The Little Foot is a ¼"-wide foot that fits many machines.) To test your ¼" seam, take a scrap piece of fabric and fold it in half, align the raw edges with the edge of the presser foot, stitch the seam, and then measure the result.

You may choose to place a piece of masking tape ¼" to the right of the needle on the throat plate to act as a guide.

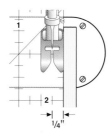

ELIMINATE BULK

THIS IS A trick you're going to love! This pressing method eliminates bulky seams magically and works on any four-patch block or other unit or block where four straight seams meet. After you have joined the four seams, place your thumbs on the darker fabric seam with one thumb on either side of the intersection. Push gently toward the lighter squares so the seams end up opposing one another. The few stitches between your ¼" seam and the raw edge will "pop" open and the seam allowances will lie down flat.

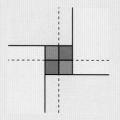

Before you begin piecing your quilt, consult your machine manual for information on how to adjust tension and stitch length. You should have no loops on either side of the stitching; adjust the tension if necessary. Set your stitch length at 12 to 15 stitches per inch.

PRESSING

To steam or not to steam is the question. Many quilters feel that using steam while pressing quilt blocks can lead to distortion. Other quilters like the nice, crisp finish that steam gives. Try pressing both with and without steam to decide which method you prefer.

CHAIN PIECING

Chain piecing is the best way to conserve not only time but also thread. To chain piece, prepare all of a particular set of pieces and feed them through the machine one after another without lifting the presser foot or stopping to snip threads. The feed dogs will catch the second piece as it comes through your machine. You can chain as many or as few pieces as you desire.

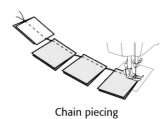

Chain piecing

APPLIQUÉ

There are two projects in this book that include appliqué: "Vision of the Future" on page 60 and "Evolution" on page 67. You can use hand or machine appliqué techniques to complete the appliqué.

Needle-Turn Appliqué

I love this hand-appliqué method most, because it's a wonderful "take along" project! Needle-turn appliqué is a method in which you use the needle to turn the seam allowance under as you stitch. If you are right-handed, it will be most comfortable to stitch in a counterclockwise direction; left-handers generally find it most comfortable to stitch in a clockwise direction.

Position and pin the appliqué to the background fabric. Thread a needle with a single strand of thread. Use the side of the needle's point to turn the fabric edge under and hold the turned-under edge in place. Guide the needle up through the background, the turned seam, and out through the top of the appliqué piece, catching just a few threads of the appliqué for the desired blind stitch. Reinsert the needle into the background fabric at about the same point where the needle came up, and turn the needle to come up again about ⅛" from the first stitch. Continue in this manner until you are all the way around the appliqué shape. Finish by taking a few tiny stitches in the background fabric behind the appliqué shape.

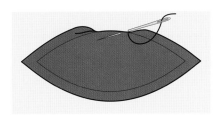

Machine Appliqué

A thin 60/8 needle will stitch through the layers easily and not leave large holes in the fabric. Refer to your machine manual for help in setting the tension and the stitch length and width.

Machine blanket-stitch appliqué. This stitch is sometimes referred to as the buttonhole stitch. I just love this stitch, because it gives an elegant finish to machine appliqué—and it's quick and easy! For this method, you can leave the edges of the appliqué shape raw. Simply hold, pin, baste, or adhere the shape to the background with fabric adhesive. Adjust the length and width of your machine stitch to achieve the look you desire, testing the results on scraps of fabric. You don't want the stitches to

stack on top of each other, but you do want them to be long enough to cover the edges of the appliqué piece.

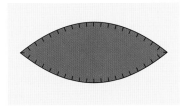

Machine blind-stitch appliqué. Blind-stitch appliqué will give you a look that most closely resembles that of hand appliqué. It is often referred to as mock hand appliqué. Select the option on your sewing machine that sews three to seven straight stitches and then a zigzag stitch. (Your manual may refer to this stitch as the blind hem stitch.) Set the stitch length to about 22 stitches per inch and the stitch width so that the zigzag takes a small "bite" into the appliqué piece. For this method, I recommend that you turn the fabric edges under ⅛" to ¼" and press using spray starch for a crisp edge to work on.

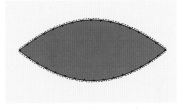

CHOOSING THREAD

SELECT A THREAD color that most closely matches the appliqué piece. If an exact match is unavailable and the background is light, choose a thread that is a shade lighter than the appliqué piece. If the background fabric is dark, select a thread that is one shade darker than the appliqué piece. Using these guidelines will keep your stitches from standing out on your finished project.

Squaring Up Blocks

Use your rotary cutter and acrylic ruler to trim equal amounts from all sides of the block or unit. Be sure to retain the ¼" seam allowances for points and to keep the design element centered in the block.

Mitered Borders

Some of the quilts in this book include borders with mitered corners. Mitered borders are a bit more challenging than borders with squared corners, but they are well worth the effort. I think mitered borders have an elegant look, and they allow the eye to move around the quilt without interruption, particularly when you are using a busy print for the border. Let's get started and wash your fears away!

1. Total the finished outside dimensions of your quilt, including the borders. Determine these numbers by measuring across the center of your quilt from side to side and adding two border widths. Add an additional 4" for seam allowances and insurance, and cut two borders to this measurement for the top and bottom borders. Measure the quilt through the center from top to bottom. Add two border widths plus 4" and cut two strips to this measurement for the side borders.

2. Fold each border in half and mark the center with a pin.

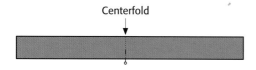

Centerfold

3. Align the center of the appropriate side of the quilt top with the center marked with a pin, right sides together. Pin well and stitch, stopping and starting ¼" from the raw edge of the quilt top. Repeat to sew all four borders to the quilt.

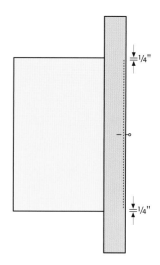

4. Place the first corner to be mitered flat on your ironing board, right side up. Fold one of the borders at a 45° angle; press. (You may need to tweak the border a bit to have it match perfectly.) Place a piece of tape over the mitered fold. Fold the quilt right sides together, aligning the border edges. Beginning with a backstitch at the border seam, stitch on the creased line, taking care not to sew through the tape. Remove the tape and press the border seams toward the borders.

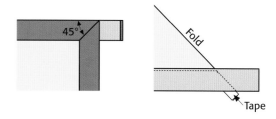

5. Trim the seam allowance on the mitered corner to ¼". Press the mitered seam open and—*ta da*—you have a mitered corner! Repeat for the next three corners. Good luck!

BACKING

The backing fabric should measure 2" larger than the quilt top on all sides. If your quilt is wider than a width of fabric (40" after laundering and removing the selvages), you will need to piece two or more lengths to achieve the necessary width. The seams can run either vertically or horizontally, whichever makes best use of the fabric.

You can make your backing from a single fabric, or you can make a pieced backing with scraps left over from your quilt top. Sometimes I like to incorporate my label into the backing.

SANDWICHING AND BASTING THE QUILT

Basting secures the three layers of your quilt to minimize or eliminate shifting as you quilt your desired design.

When preparing to baste your quilt, place the backing, right side down, on a hard surface. (Wood floors, linoleum floors, or large tables are perfect for this.) Smooth out any wrinkles, moving from the center to the edges so there are no wrinkles or puckers in the fabric, and tape securely. (I prefer the blue painter's tape found at any hardware store.) Center the batting over the backing, again smoothing out as you go. Next, layer your pressed quilt top, right side up. You are now ready to baste.

For hand quilting, start in the center of the quilt and use light-colored thread to baste a grid of vertical and horizontal lines approximately 3" to 4" apart. Finish by basting around the outside edges.

For machine quilting, substitute small, rustproof safety pins for the thread, and try to avoid areas such as seams where you expect to quilt.

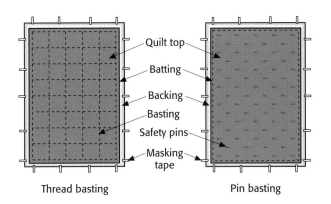

Thread basting   Pin basting

MAKING AND ADDING BINDING

1. Trim the binding fabric to make a square. (For example, trim ¾ yard of fabric to make a 27" x 27" square.) On the wrong side of the fabric, mark the top and bottom with chalk. Cut the fabric in half on the diagonal. Sew the two triangles together with a ¼" seam along the marked edges as shown. Press the seams open.

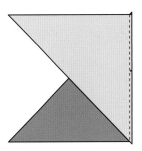

2. On the wrong side of the unit from step 1, mark parallel diagonal lines 2½" apart. Trim off any dog-ears.

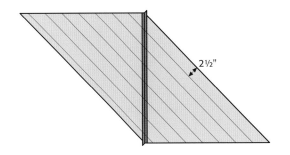

2½"

3. Bring the right sides of the nonbias edges together to make a tube. Match the lines, offsetting them by one width, and sew with a ¼" seam. Press the seam open and cut along the lines to make a continuous bias strip.

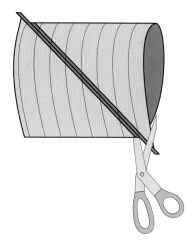

4. Trim the beginning end of the binding strip at a 45° angle, turn the angled edge under ⅜", and press. Fold the strip in half lengthwise, wrong sides together, and press.

Fold line

5. Trim the batting and batting even with the edges of the quilt top. Align the raw edges of the binding and quilt top. Leaving the first 6" free, and starting in the middle of a side (not a corner), start sewing the binding to the quilt with a ¼" seam as shown. (I like to use a walking foot, because it helps feed the layers evenly.) Stop stitching ¼" from the corner.

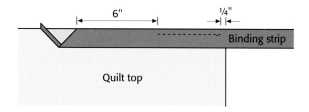

6"   ¼"

Binding strip

Quilt top

6. Fold the binding up, making a 45° angle as shown.

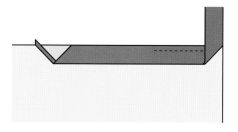

7. Fold the binding down, aligning it with the adjacent edge, and begin stitching from the corner. Repeat for all remaining corners.

8. Stop stitching with the needle down about 12" before reaching the beginning of your binding. Trim the tail of the binding, leaving about 6" beyond the beginning diagonal edge. Insert the cut edge of binding into the beginning diagonal edge, and complete the seam, backstitching at the overlap.

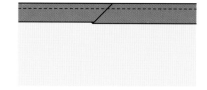

RESOURCES

For bottles, jars, and vials:
SKS Bottle & Packaging Inc.
3 Knabner Rd.
Mechanicville, NY 12118
518-899-7488
www.sks-bottle.com

Specialty Bottle LLC
5215 5th Ave. S
Seattle, WA 98108
206-340-0459
www.specialtybottle.com

For buckwheat hulls ("Buckwheat Eye Mask" on page 52):
True Foods Market
517 West 100 North
Providence, UT 84332
435-755-9266
www.truefoodsmarket.com

For citric acid ("Tea Rose Bath Bombs" on page 38), essential oils, and molds:
Soap Crafters Company
2944 S. West Temple
Salt Lake City, UT 84115
801-484-5121
www.soapcrafters.com

For essential oils:
Saidel Inc.
18724 109th Lane SE
Renton, WA 98055
877-781-1112
www.aromatherapywebsite.com

For Zen Garden spa products (used in location photography):
The Quilted Dragon
11124 Gravelly Lake Dr. SW
Lakewood, WA 98499
253-582-7455
www.quilted-dragon.com

ACKNOWLEDGMENTS

THERE IS NO way that I can take all the credit for this book. Many people have touched my life, and I want to thank all of you from the bottom of my heart.

First and foremost to the love of my life, Jack! There are no words to tell you how much you do for me. I adore you and could never have done this had it not been for your encouragement, support, and undying patience and love.

To my children, Brittany and Nicholas, for the lessons I learn every day from each of you. You are blessings in my life daily!

Thank-you isn't enough to say to my parents, Mimi and Jack Teters. I love you both so much!

Special thanks to Sally Harrington. You are one of my best cheerleaders—a confidant and wonderful sounding board.

To QuiltFriends, an online quilting group composed of quilters from all over the world. You have given a wealth of inspiration, opinions, hugs, and constant prayers. Some put many hours into the sewing of the quilt tops, some quilted for me, and—most of all—you have been dear friends.

To my "binding angels," Lana Russ, Lois Anderson, Sally Harrington, Mimi Teters, Brittany Zeigler, Cora Tunberg, and Jo Uhlman—the time you gave is priceless!

To the Group Health Cooperative Quilters, who supported and cheered me on.

To the Alexis Hotel in Seattle, Washington, for providing one of their Spa Suites and the John Lennon Suite as locations for our photo shoot, with huge thanks to Katharine Dooley and her fabulous staff.

To Joe and Becky Scellato of the Quilted Dragon for the Zen bath and body products used in the photo shoot.

And a special tribute to my late grandmother, Vivian Marie Teters: the memories and love she left for me continue to be a positive force and inspiration in my life.

ABOUT THE AUTHOR

Photo by Marie Martineau, Timeless Treasures Photography

Julia Teters-Zeigler was an art major in college, where she met the love of her life, married, and started her family. She enjoyed smocking when her children were babies and continues to dabble in knitting, painting, and scrapbooking, but her true passion has always been quilting.

Julia currently works at the Quilted Dragon in Lakewood, Washington. She teaches and has a small pattern business. She is a member of the Association of Pacific Northwest Quilters, a charter member of the Washington Stars Quilt Guild, a member of the Comforters Quilt Guild, and a charter member of Quilters by the Bay.

With children grown, Julia and her husband, Jack, are empty nesters in Olympia, Washington. You can learn more at Julia's Web site, www.just-julia.com.

Each day comes bearing its own gifts. Untie the ribbons.
—RUTH ANN SCHABACKER